THE
MODERN CLASS BOOK

OF

FRENCH PRONUNCIATION,

CONTAINING

ALL THE RULES, WITH THEIR EXCEPTIONS, WHICH GOVERN
THE PRONUNCIATION OF THE FRENCH LANGUAGE.

With an Appendix,

IN WHICH THE CONJUGATION OF THE MOST DIFFICULT VERBS IS GIVEN,
TOGETHER WITH THE NUMBERS, MONTHS, DAYS OF THE WEEK,
ETC., ETC., WITH THE WRITTEN PRONUNCIATION.

BY V. ALVERGNAT,

TEACHER OF THE FRENCH LANGUAGE IN THE HARTFORD HIGH SCHOOL.

BOSTON:
SCHOENHOF AND MOELLER,
Publishers and Importers,
40 WINTER STREET.
1872.

Entered according to Act of Congress, in the year 1872, by
V. ALVERGNAT,
In the Office of the Librarian of Congress, at Washington.

CAMBRIDGE:
PRESS OF JOHN WILSON AND SON.

PREFACE.

OF the three principal points of the comprehensive study of the French language, — viz., *pronunciation, grammar,* and the *acquisition of a vocabulary,* — the first in order and most important is PRONUNCIATION. But, while grammars have been multiplied almost beyond necessity, text-books on French pronunciation are few, and none of them complete.

Of the usefulness, nay, of the indispensability, of a complete and accurate class-book of French pronunciation, it is unnecessary to speak: every teacher and pupil has felt the need of it. How many, even among the best French scholars, for want of a proper book of reference for rules and exceptions so easily forgotten, have been (sometimes for years) feeling their way in the dark!

With the hope, and prompted by the desire, of helping the student in securing a pure and correct pronunciation, I have attempted to supply a deficiency which I have sorely felt myself at every step of my teaching.

Much might be said in favor of the modern system of spelling adhered to in the present work. Suffice it to state that it is no new method. Introduced in French schools more than thirty years ago, it has superseded the old and unnatural way of spelling words, *for their pronunciation,* by naming each one of their letters, silent or not. In the modern system, the *sounds* only are named; and, as their names are but duplicates of the sounds, a correct pronunciation of any assemblage of sounds (or syllables) must necessarily follow.

With the exception of the two vowel-sounds generally represented by *eu* and *un*, which have no exact equivalent in English, ALL French sounds have representatives in the English language, — a fact which will be satisfactorily demonstrated in the course of the lessons. Now let the English word which possesses the *true* French sound be once fixed in the mind of the pupil, and it is both natural and easy for him to emit that sound in its perfection.

Upon this self-evident fact my method is based; and certainly no other is simpler, better, more natural, practical, and expeditious.

In the preparation of this book, I have availed myself of all the sources of information within my reach, and followed the best authorities. The works of J. MAIGNE, G. H. AUBERTIN, A. FÉLINE, P. LAROUSSE, &c., and particularly the recent exhaustive treatise of French pronunciation by M. A. LESAINT, have afforded me much help on doubtful points. In short, I have spared neither time, trouble, nor expense to make this work the standard text-book of French pronunciation.

Hoping that my labors have not been in vain, I now leave the work to the appreciation of teachers and students.

V. ALVERGNAT.

HARTFORD, CONN., July, 1872.

CONTENTS.

	PAGE
PREFACE	iii
KEY TO PRONUNCIATION	2
LESSONS	3
VOWEL-SOUNDS AND ACCENTS	6
NASAL SOUNDS	12
CONSONANTS	14, 72
VOWEL-LETTERS AND SOUNDS	24
DIPHTHONGS	60
CONSONANTS	14, 72
APPENDIX	127
THE MARSEILLAISE HYMN	164
LA MARSEILLAISE (Music)	170

THE MODERN CLASS-BOOK

OF

FRENCH PRONUNCIATION.

KEY TO THE PRONUNCIATION.

VOWEL SOUNDS.

Conventional Characters.				French Sounds.
1. ă,	as a	in as	. . . . .	a short.
2. { ah,	,, a	,, father	. . . .	a semi-long.
āh,	,, a	,, father	. . . .	â long.
3. uh,	,, e	,, ermine	. . .	e guttural.
4. ĕ,	,, e	,, move	. . . .	e semi-mute.*
5. a,	,, a	,, late	. . . .	é acute.
6. { eh,	,, e	,, met	. . . .	è grave.
ēh,	,, e	,, there	. . . .	ê long.
7. ee,	,, i	,, police	. . . .	i short.
8. ŏ,	,, o	,, nor	. . . .	o short.
9. { o,	,, o	,, also	. . . .	o semi-long.
ō,	,, o	,, no	. . . . .	ô long.
10. ŭ,	,, u	,, constitution	. .	u, û, short and long.
11. eū,	,, i	,, first	. . . .	eu semi-long.
12. oo,	,, oo	,, too	. . . .	ou semi-long.

NASAL SOUNDS.

13. āñ,	as an	in want	. . . .	an semi-long.
14. īñ,	,, an	,, Yankee	. . .	in semi-long.
15. ōñ,	,, on	,, don't	. . . .	on semi-long.
16. ūñ,	,, un	,, grunt	. . . .	un semi-long.

IRREGULAR DIPHTHONGS.

17. weh,	as wea	in wear	. . . .	oi semi-long.
18. wah,	,, wa	,, water	. . .	oi open.

ARTICULATED SOUNDS.

ḡ,	as g	in go	. . . .	g hard.
zh,	,, z	,, glazier	. . . . .	g soft.
ḡñ,	,, ng	,, singing	. . . . .	g liquid.
ȳ,	,, y	,, yes	. . . .	l liquid.

---

* The semi-mute e sound will also be represented by an apostrophe (thus, ') when the sound which e represents is a nearly inaudible breathing.

THE MODERN CLASS-BOOK

OF

FRENCH PRONUNCIATION.

FIRST LESSON. *Première leçon.*

LETTERS.

1. The French alphabet was originally composed of twenty-five letters. Now, by the *intrusion* of w, borrowed from the alphabet of Northern nations, it contains twenty-six letters.

2. The modern names of the French letters correspond, as nearly as possible, to the sounds which they represent.

		Called	Pronounced as in			Called	Pronounced as in
1.	a	ah	father.	14.	n	nuh	nut.
2.	b	buh	budge.	15.	o	o	obedience.
3.	c	kuh	cuttle.	16.	p	puh	purr.
4.	d	duh	dutch.	17.	q	kuh	piquet.
5.	e	uh	ermine.	18.	r	ruh	runner.
6.	f	fuh	fudge.	19.	s	suh	subject.
7.	g	guh	gun.	20.	t	tuh	tusk.
8.	h	uh	herb.	21.	u	u	constitution.
9.	i	ee	police.	22.	v	vuh	vulture.
10.	j	zhuh	z in azure.	23.	w	vuh	vulture.
11.	k	kuh	kernel.	24.	x	gzuh	exult.
12.	l	luh	luggage.	25.	y	ee	i in police.
13.	m	muh	must.	26.	z	zuh	zurlite.

OBSERVATION.—w is generally called *double v;* and y, *i grec.*

THEORY.

I. OBS.—j, k, q, r, v, z, are the only letters whose pronunciation never varies. Each one of the other letters represents two or more sounds, according to place and circumstances, and therefore has different names.

II. OBS.—The letter u is the only one whose pronunciation presents some difficulty to the beginner. It is true that a compatatively large number of Americans pronounce the u of *constitution* and *duenna* as accurately as the most fastidious Frenchman could desire. But the bare statement of this fact being insufficient in itself to enable the learner to pronounce the French u correctly, I give here an easy method for the acquisition of that sound. If my directions are faithfully followed, failure will be impossible.

DIRECTIONS.—Pronounce loudly, and as distinctly as you can, the sound represented by ee in *lee*. Now, as soon as you have fairly started the ee sound, let your lips gently advance, as if you were intending to whistle, bring them nearer and nearer together until only a *very narrow* opening is left for the passage of the sounding breath. Meanwhile be very careful not to move your tongue. The whole operation must be accomplished while the ee sound is in process of emission.

As you proceed, you will observe a gradual change in the quality of the sound. You should not stop then; but continue as long as your breath lasts, in order to perfect the operation. The inevitable result will be the transformation of the ee sound into that of the French u.

You should try again until your ear is accustomed to the new sound, carefully guarding against stiffness or rigidity in your lips: their gradual motion should be natural and easy.

LETTERS. 5

PRACTICE.

FIRST EXERCISE. *Premier exercice.*

A, b, c, d, e, f, g, h, i, j, k, l, m, n, o,
ah buh kuh duh uh fuh guh uh ee zhuh kuh luh muh nuh o

p, q, r, s, t, u, v, w, x, y, z, a, e, i, o, u, y,
puh kuh ruh suh tuh u vuh vuh gzuh ee zuh ah uh ee o u ee

z, x, w, v, t, s, r, q, p, n, m, l, k, j, h, g, f, d,
zuh gzuh vuh vuh tuh suh ruh kuh puh nuh muh luh kuh zhuh uh guh fuh duh

c, b, y, u, o, i, e, a, l, w, z, m, a, x, u, b, n,
kuh buh ee u o ee uh ah luh vuh zuh muh ah gzuh u buh nuh

k, o, d, v, j, e, p, t, h, f, q, s, g, r, i, c, j, m,
kuh o duh vuh zhuh uh puh tuh uh fuh kuh suh guh ruh ee kuh zhuh muh

b, n, y, v, k, z, p, t, u, o, d, w, x, l, n, e, a.
buh nuh ee vuh kuh zuh puh tuh u o duh vuh gzuh luh nuh uh ah

---

A, b, c, d, e, f, g, h, i, j, k, l, m, n, o, p, q,

r, s, t, u, v, w, x, y, z, a, e, i, o, u, y, z, x, w,

v, t, s, r, q, p, n, m, l, k, j, h, g, f, d, k, b, y,

u, o, i, e, a, l, w, z, m, a, x, u, b, n, k, o, d, v,

j, e, p, t, h, f, q, s, g, r, i, c, j, m, b, n, y, v,

k, z, p, t, u, o, d, w, x, l, n, e, a.

NOTE. — The first part of this and the following exercises might be covered up with a sheet of paper while the learner is reading the second part.

THEORY.

SECOND LESSON. *Deuxième leçon.*

3. The French alphabet is divided into six vowels and twenty consonants.

4. The vowels are:

a, e, i, o, u, y.

5. The consonants or articulations are:

b, c, d, f, g, h, j, k, l, m, n, p, q, r, s, t, v, w, x, z.

VOWEL-SOUNDS AND ACCENTS.

6. *A vowel-sound is the sonorous emission of breath*, which can be modulated into a, e, i, o, u, &c.

OBS. — The six vowel-letters do not represent all the modifications of which the sounding breath is susceptible.

This deficiency of particular characters to represent each one of our eighteen vowel-sounds is supplied partly by combinations of letters, and partly by some orthographical signs, called *accents*.

7. These accents, three in number, are:

1. The *acute* ('), inclined from right to left.
2. The *grave* (`), inclined from left to right.
3. The *circumflex* (^), a combination of the other two.

8. These accents alter the sound of the letter over which they are placed, both in quality and quantity.

OBS. — The quantity of a sound is the extent of its duration, — the length of time required for its complete emission.

9. Accents are used, also, as signs of distinction between words containing the same letters, but having a different meaning. Examples: a, *has;* à, *to;* ou, *or;* où, *where;* &c.

THEORY.

THE FIFTEEN FORMS OF THE VOWEL-LETTERS.

a, à, â; e, é, è, ê; i, î; o, ô; u, ù, û; y.

OBS.— As will be seen, the acute accent is used only with the letter e.

THE EIGHTEEN FRENCH VOWEL-SOUNDS, WITH THEIR ENGLISH EQUIVALENTS.

1. a, à, like a in as.
2. â, ,, a ,, father.
3. e, ,, e ,, ermine.
4. e, ,, e ,, move.
5. é, ,, a ,, late (nearly).
6. è, like e in met.
7. i, î, y, ,, i ,, police.
8. o, ,, o ,, nor.
9. ô, ,, o ,, no.
10. u, û, ,, u ,, constitution.

11. eu, like i in first (nearly). | 12. ou, like oo in too.

NASAL SOUNDS.

13. an, like an in want.
14. in, ,, an ,, Yankee.
15. on, like on in don't.
16. un, ,, un ,, grunt.

IRREGULAR SOUNDS.

17. oi, oy, like wea in wear. | 18. oi, like wa in water.*

OBS.— The first ten sounds are the only ones that can be represented by single letters.

---

* There are, it is true, other shades in sounds, of which a very minute and mathematical division and gradation might be made: as many as forty modifications in sounds have been recognized. But, for all practical purposes, the eighteen given above have been found amply sufficient. Nevertheless, what may be interesting and useful to the student on this subject will be presented at the proper time and place.

THEORY.

10. Thirteen of our consonants, viz., b, d, f, k, l, m, n, p, r, s, t, v, z, when at the beginning of words, are pronounced in French as they are in English.

SYLLABIFICATION.

11. *French words are divided upon a vowel-sound;* hence when a consonant is single between two vowels it begins the syllable. Thus, **page, bile, sofa,** have two syllables, — *pa-ge, bi-le, so-fa;* **image, opéra,** have three, — *i-ma-ge, o-pé-ra;* **fatalité, capitale,** four syllables, — *fa-ta-li-té, ca-pi-ta-le;* **imaginera,** five, — *i-ma-gi-ne-ra;* &c.

12. To this rule there are but few exceptions. Some words are divided according to etymology; but, as far as *pronunciation* is concerned, the above rule holds good in all cases.

13. When two or more consonants occur between two vowels, the division is, generally, as in English, between the consonants.

THE FINAL E.

14. When the final e is preceded by a consonant, as in **type, âge, table, obole,** &c., it is called semi-mute, and represents nothing more than a scarcely audible emission of breath, which disappears with the vanishing sound of the preceding consonant. This semi-mute e represents the faintest of our vowel-sounds, similar in all respects to the English e sound of *tape, zone, move,* &c.

PRACTICE.

SECOND EXERCISE.*   *Deuxième exercice.*

La va-ni-té, lă vă nee ta.	the vanity.	Le do-mi-no, luh dŏ mee no.	the domino.
dé-fi, so-fa, da fee, sŏ fă.	challenge, sofa.	le dé-pu-té, luh da pü ta.	the deputy.
po-li, do-du, pŏ lee, dŏ dü.	polished, plump.	la vé-ri-té, lă va ree ta.	the truth.
le pâ-té, ti-ré, luh păh ta, tee ra.	the pie, drawn.	le rô-ti, luh ro tee.	the roast-meat.
le me-nu, luh muh nü.	the bill of fare.	pa-no-ra-ma, pă nŏ ră mă.	panorama.
fi-dé-li-té, fee da lee ta.	faithfulness.	mo-ra-li-té, mŏ ră lee ta.	morality.
le la-va-bo, luh lă vă bo.	the washstand.	le to-ry, za-ra, luh tŏ ree, ză ră.	the tory, zara.

La vanité, défi, sofa, poli, dodu, le pâté, tiré, le menu, fidélité, le lavabo, le domino, le député, la vérité, le roti, panorama, moralité, le tory, zara.

---

* See "Key to the Pronunciation," at the beginning of the book; also at the bottom of this page.

In the MODERN FRENCH METHOD OF SPELLING FOR PRONUNCIATION (which must naturally be adopted by foreigners for spelling French words), —

1. The consonant is named. 2. The vowel-sound is uttered, which is represented by the vowel or by the assemblage of letters annexed to that consonant. 3. The syllabic sound is now given distinctly.

In the case of polysyllabic words, each successive syllable will, of course, be treated in the same manner; but the first is repeated, and joined to the second when the latter has been spelled; and these two syllables, likewise, to the third; and so on. Thus **La vanité** will be spelled: luh ă lă; vuh ă vă, nuh ee nee, vănee; tuh a ta, văneeta; lă văneeta. **Défi** will be spelled: duh a da, fuh ee fee, dafee; &c.

ă, as; ah, âh, father; uh, ermine; ŏ or ', move; a, late; eh, met; ēh, there; ee, police; ŏ, nor; o, also; ō, no; ŭ, constitution.

THEORY.

THIRD LESSON.   *Troisième leçon.*

THE *EU* SOUND.

15. It is difficult to define the 11th sound, because it has no (recognized) exact equivalent in English. Mere words cannot convey a correct idea of its mixed nature, which partakes of that of **e** in "**ermine**," and of **u** in "**constitution**," completing a scale of three sounds which the student can learn in five minutes from a native, but which it is almost impossible to represent on paper.

But, although not recognized as an element of the English pronunciation, this sound is nevertheless pretty correctly uttered by persons who pronounce the word **first** with protruding and somewhat contracted lips. Here the **i** sound closely resembles the **eu** sound of the French.

OBS.—In order to pronounce the **eu** sound correctly, the mouth should form a sort of funnel, holding back the superabundance of the sonorous air, which, being supplied by the lungs faster than it can escape, produces, at its exit through the small opening of the lips, the somewhat obscure but compact and harmonious **eu** sound.*

---

* Let the student, after having substituted the sound of **e** in **ermine** for that of **ee** in **lee**, repeat the operation prescribed on page 4 for the pronunciation of **u**, and the sound ultimately produced will be the French **eu** sound (11th in our scale).

PRACTICE.

THIRD EXERCISE.   *Troisième exercice.*

¹La ⁸ro-⁴be,* ⁷ri-⁴de,	the gown, wrinkle.	
lă rŏb', reed'.		
¹⁰u-⁴ne ⁷pi-⁴le, ¹⁰lu-⁴ne,	a heap, moon.	
ŭn' peel', lŭn'.		
³le ⁷ty-⁴pe, ⁶pè-¹re,	the type, father.	
luh teep', pĕhr'.		
¹⁰mû-⁴re, ³le ¹⁰tu-⁴be,	ripe, the tube.	
mūr', luh tūb'.		
⁶pê-⁴le—⁶mê-⁴le,	pell-mell.	
pĕhl' - mĕhl'.		
¹la ⁸vo-⁴le, ⁹mô-⁴le,	the vole, pier.	
lă vŏl', mōl'.		
¹la ⁸no-⁴ne, ¹⁰du-⁴pe,	the nun, dupe.	
lă nŏn,' dŭp'.		

⁵é-¹¹meu-⁴te, ¹¹feu,	riot, fire.	
a mēut', fēu.		
³le ⁸ne-¹¹veu, ³le ¹²sou,	the nephew, the [penny.	
luh nuh vēu, luh soo.		
¹a-¹ma-¹²dou,	German tinder.	
ă mă doo.		
¹⁰u-⁴ne ¹¹meu-⁴te,	a pack of hounds.	
ŭn' mēut'.		
³le ¹ma-¹la-⁴de,	the sick one.	
luh mă lăd'.		
¹la ¹pa-⁸ro-⁴le,	the word.	
lă pă rŏl'.		
¹²dou-⁴ze, ⁵Pé-¹²rou,	twelve, Peru.	
dooz', pă roo.		

La robe, ride, une pile, lune, le type, père, mûre, le tube, pêle-mêle, la vole, môle, la none, dupe, émeute, feu, le neveu, le sou, amadou, une meute, le malade, la parole, douze, Pérou.

---

* In spelling words ending with a semi-mute syllable, the student, having to name the final **e**, will call it **uh**; and, in pronouncing the final syllable *alone*, he will retain that **uh** sound for greater convenience. Thus, the last syllable of **robe** will be spelled, buh uh buh; but, in joining the two syllables for the enunciation of the whole word, the sound uh must necessarily be dismissed: the voice dwells upon the b sound, which absorbs the faint breathing represented by the semi-mute e. Robe will therefore be spelled: ruh ŏ rŏ, buh uh buh, rŏb'; and **émeute**: a, muh ēū mēū, amēū; tuh uh tuh; amēūt'.

OBS. — In the written pronunciation throughout this book, this semi-mute e sound is represented either by the conventional character ĕ, or simply by an apostrophe (').

ă, as; ah, äh, father; uh, ermine; ĕ or ', move; a, late; eh, met; ēh, there; ee, police; ŏ, nor; o, also; ō, no; ŭ, constitution; ēū, first; oo, too.

THEORY.

FOURTH LESSON. *Quatrième leçon.*

THE NASAL SOUNDS.

16. From the peculiarity of their formation, these sounds present also some difficulty in the way of conveying a clear idea of their true nature; not because they do not exist in English, but because, like the **eu** sound, they are not recognized as elements of its pronunciation.

I will presently demonstrate that three of our four nasal sounds are fairly represented in some English expressions.

For instance, when **I don't want to** is spoken with great emphasis, the stress of the voice resting upon the word **want**, our first nasal sound is uttered in *all its* purity. Let us see: —

If the student pronounce **I don't want to** with force and decision, he will notice that the **t** of **want** is not sounded at all: only one **t** sound is heard, — that of **to**. Let him now drop that word **to**, and pronounce **wan**(t) precisely as he did before, and he will perceive that not only the *t*, but the *n* also, of *want* is silent. Next, let him dismiss **I don't**, and finally, dropping the **w** sound, utter the now isolated, accidental sound represented by **a** of *wa*(*nt*). That sound, if the operation has been carefully performed, will be identical with the first French nasal sound (13th in our scale).

17. Likewise in **Yankee**, the sound represented by **an is an** exact equivalent to our second nasal sound (14th).

18. In **don't**, said with earnestness, the **on** sound is absolutely the same as the French nasal sound (15th) represented by that combination.

19. The **un** in **grunt** is a pretty fair representative of our fourth nasal sound (16th in the scale).

OBS. — These last three sounds can easily be obtained by a process similar to that prescribed for the acquisition of the first (§ 16).

PRACTICE.

FOURTH EXERCISE.   *Quatrième exercice.*

Un din-don,* ŭṉ diṉ dōṉ.	a turkey.	Meu-don, a-veu, meū dōṉ, ă veū.	Meudon, con-[fession.
u-ne ban-de, ŭn' bāṉd'.	a band.	in-di-vi-du, iṉ dee vee dŭ.	individual.
la man-do-li-ne, lă māṉ dŏ leen'.	the mandolin.	un ta-ma-rin, ŭṉ tă mă rīṉ.	a tamarind-tree.
la dan-se, lă dāṉs'.	the dance.	le ty-ran, luh tee rāṉ.	the tyrant.
le pa-la-tin, luh pă lă' tīṉ.	the palatine.	i-non-dé, ee nōṉ da.	flooded.
le lun-di, luh lŭṉ dee.	on Monday.	un po-ti-ron, ŭṉ pŏ tee rōṉ.	a pumpkin.
u-ne son-de, ŭn' sōṉd'.	a sounding-line.	a-ban-don, ă bāṉ dōṉ.	abandonment.

Un dindon, une bande, la mandoline, la danse, le palatin, le lundi, une sonde, Meudon, aveu, individu, un tamarin, le tyran, inondé, un potiron, abandon.

---

* **Un dindon** will be spelled: **ŭṉ**; duh **īṉ dīṉ**, duh **ōṉ dōṉ, dīṉ-dōṉ**; **ŭṉ dīṉdōṉ**.

OBS.— The student will carefully guard against the natural tendency to sound the n. The tongue must absolutely lie flat and motionless as long as the nasal sound lasts. The least infraction of this rule would inevitably defeat the object in view.

In the formation of the nasal sounds, the peculiarity is that the air from the lungs is thrown into the pharyngeal and nasal cavities, and, striking their resounding membranous walls, produces that sort of obscure sonority which so much resembles the nasal ringing, or twang, which characterizes the pronunciation of New-England country people.

ă, as; ab, äh, father; uh, ermine; ĕ or ', move; a, late; eh, met; ēh, there; ee, police; ŏ, nor; o, also; ō, no; ŭ, constitution; eū, first; oo, too; āṉ, want; īṉ, Yankee; ōṉ, don't; ūṉ, grunt.

THEORY.

FIFTH LESSON. *Cinquième leçon.*

THE TWO IRREGULAR SOUNDS.

20. The 17th vowel-sound, which is generally represented by **oi** and **oy**, is similar to the sound of **wea** in *wear*.

21. The 18th is also represented by **oi**, and is identical with the sound of **wa** in *water*. It occurs in the following ten words only: *bois, mois, pois, poids, empois, noix, noisette, trois, troisième, troisièmement.*

OBS. — The 17th and 18th vowel-sounds are also considered as irregular diphthongs.

GENERAL RULE. — The acute e (short ĕ of the Latin) and the vowel-letters used without accents represent short sounds; the grave accent indicates a semi-long sound; and, with a few exceptions, the circumflex accent (mark of contraction) characterizes the longest vowel-sounds.

CONSONANTS.

REMARKS. — As nations attain a higher degree of civilization and refinement, the asperities of their language, little by little, disappear. The guttural, and the harsher and more discordant, consonant sounds, particularly at the end of words, are gradually slighted, and ultimately dropped altogether; the voice naturally seeking to rest upon the softer and more pleasant vowel-sounds. The ear, also, becoming more delicate, would be offended by the continual occurrence of coarse and unnecessarily energetic sounds, and requires a more frequent use of the smooth and harmonious vowel-sounds.

In French this process of softening the pronunciation has been carried to a greater extent than in other languages; and, as a great number of words thus altered in their pronunciation have retained their old orthography, it follows that nearly all the final consonants are silent in our language.

22. However, **b, c, f, l, q,** and **r**, final, are still sounded in almost all the words which they terminate.

PRACTICE.

FIFTH EXERCISE. *Cinquième exercice.*

La foi, la poi-re, the faith, the pear.
lă fweh, lă pwehr'.

vou-loir,* toi-le, to wish, linen.
voo lwehr', twehl'.

u-ne voi-tu-re, a carriage.
ŭn' vweh tŭr'.

la soif,* moi, the thirst, me.
lă swehf, mwah.

la mé-moi-re, the memory.
lă ma mwehr'.

le mois, noix, the month, nut.
luh mwah, nwah.

du bois, le pois, some wood, the [pea.
dŭ bwah, luh pwah.

un poids,* soi, a weight, one's [self.
ŭn pwah, sweh.

Em-pois, boî-te, starch, box.
ăṁ pwah, bwĕht'.

la voi-lu-re, the set of sails
lă vweh lŭr'.

un dé-vi-doir, a reel.
ŭn dă vee dwehr.

sa-voir, poil, to know, hair.
să vwehf, pwehl.

bé-nir, bâ-tir, to bless, to build
ba neer, băh teer.

le dé-funt, the deceased.
luh da fŭṅ.

sou-pir, bol, sigh, bowl.
soo peer, bŏl.

Fond-du-Lac, Fond-du-Lac.
foṅ dŭ lăk.

La foi, la poire, vouloir, toile, une voiture, la soif, moi, la mémoire, le mois, noix, du bois, le pois, un poids, soi, empois, boîte, la voilure, un dévidoir, savoir, poil, bénir, bâtir, le défunt, soupir, bol, Fond-du-Lac.

---

* Vouloir, la soif, un poids, will be spelled: vuh oo voo, luh weh ruh lwehr, voolwehr; luh ă lă, suh weh fuh swehf, lă swehf; ŭṅ, puh wah pwah, ŭṅ pwah; &c.

ă, as; ah, ăh, father; uh, ermine; ŏ or ', move; a, late; eh, met; ĕh, there; ee, police; ŏ, nor; o, also; ō, no; ŭ, constitution; ēu, first; oo, too; āṅ, want; īṅ, Yankee; ōṅ, don't; ūṅ, grunt; weh, wear; wah, water.

THEORY.

SIXTH LESSON. *Sixième leçon.*

CONSONANTS.

23. r final, in polysyllabic words, is silent when it is immediately preceded by e.*

24. GENERAL RULE. — The final consonants of proper names and words of foreign origin are fully sounded.

25. When a consonant not final nor double terminates a syllable, it is generally sounded.

Ex. — **falourde, piste**, are pronounced *fàloord', peest'*.

C.

26. c is called *kuh*, and is sounded as **k** in *key* before a, o, u, l, n, r, t, œ, œi; also when final.

27. c is silent before q or another c joined to the vowels a, o, u, or to the consonants l, r. The final c is also silent after a nasal sound.

Ex. — **le banc** is pronounced *luh bān*.

28. c has the soft sound of s in *so*, and is called *suh* before e, i, and y.

29. ç (with the cedilla) is used only before a, o, u, and has also the soft sound of s in *so*.

30. The cedilla (¸), which is used with the c only, is an indication of the soft sound s, and therefore acts as a preventive against the hard sound *kuh*.

---

* The French r is either strongly articulated or altogether silent. There is a marked difference between the French and the English language in the pronunciation of that consonant. In English, the r is distinctly pronounced at the beginning of words only. In the middle and at the end of words it is generally slurred, — gliding into an insignificant sound; as in *iron, myrrh, cur*, &c.

In French, when the r is sounded, it is strongly rolled and fully articulated with even greater force than in the English word *roaring*.

PRACTICE.

SIXTH EXERCISE. *Sixième exercice.*

Le bo-cal, luh bŏ kăl.	the glass-bowl.	Ca-fé, ca-duc, kă fa, kă dŭk.	coffee, decrepit.
la fa-ça-de, lă fă săd'.	the frontage.	bé-né-di-ci-té, ba na dee see ta.	benediction.
un co-lo-nel, ŭn kŏ lŏ nehl.	a colonel.	oc-cul-te, ŏ. kŭlt'.	occult.
bé-né-fi-ce, ba na fees'.	benefit.	il suc-cé-da, eel sŭk sa dă.	he did succeed.
me-na-çons, muh nă sōn.	let us threaten.	Ca-lyp-so, kă leep so.	Calypso.
u-ne pin-ce, ŭn' pīns'.	a pair of pincers.	le ma-ca-ron, luh mă kă rōn.	the macaroon.
la le-çon, lă luh sōn.	the lesson.	ca-ra-va-ne, kă ră văn'.	caravan.
la cul-bu-te, lă kŭl bŭt'.	the somersault.	sa ca-ba-ne, să kă băn'.	his cabin.
suc-cur-sa-le, sŭ kŭr săl'.	branch office.	un ca-na-pé, ŭn kă nă pa.	a sofa.

Le bocal, la façade, un colonel, bénéfice, menaçons, une pince, la leçon, la culbute, succursale, café, caduc, bénédicité, occulte, il succéda, Calypso, le macaron, caravane, sa cabane, un canapé,

---

ă, as; ah, äh, father; uh, ermine; ĕ or ', move; a, late; eh, met; ēh, there; ee, police; ŏ, nor; o, also; ō, no; ŭ, constitution; ēū, first; oo, too; a͞n, want; i͞n, Yankee; o͞n, don't; u͞n, grunt; weh, wear; wah, water.

THEORY.

SEVENTH LESSON. *Septième leçon.*

CONSONANTS.

G.

31. g is sounded as in *go, fig,* before **a, o, u, l, m, r, d**; and is called *guh.*

32. Before **e, i, y**, it has the soft sound of **z** in *glazier;* and is called *zhuh.*

33. In **gu** preceding **e, i,** or **y**, the **u** is silent, being used merely as an orthographic letter to indicate that the **g** retains its hard sound (as in *go*).

H.

34. The French **h,** called "aspirate" and "mute," is *never sounded,* and, like all other silent letters, is not named in spelling for pronunciation.

J.

35. **j**, which is *always* pronounced as **z** in *glazier* (precisely as **g** soft), is never doubled, never followed by another consonant, and never final in *French words.* It is used with all the vowels, but can be joined to **i** and **y** only by the elision of **e** before words beginning with those letters.

L.

36. **l** has two distinct sounds, — the natural and the liquid sounds.

37. **l** natural is sounded as in English in *level, lily.*

38. **l** liquid is pronounced as **y** in *yes, year.*

39. GENERAL RULE. — **l** is liquid when, in the same syllable, it is immediately preceded by **i**.

Q.

40. With the exception of **coq** and **cinq, q** is always followed by **u**; and the two letters **qu** are generally pronounced as **k** in *key.*

PRACTICE.

SEVENTH EXERCISE. *Septième exercice.*

Ré-gu-la-ri-té, ra gu là ree ta.	regularity.	Hô-pi-tal, ŏ pee tăl.	hospital.
tu a-ga-ças, tü ă gă să.	thou didst tease.	hor-lo-ge, ŏr lŏzh'.	time-keeper.
la rou-geo-le, lă roo zhŏl'.	the measles.	un jou-jou, ūn zhoo zhoo.	a plaything.
va-ga-bond, vă gă bōn.	vagrant.	le ju-ju-be, luh zhü zhüb'.	jujube.
un gué-ri-don, ūn ga ree dōn.	a round-table.	mon jar-din, mōn zhăr dĭn.	my garden.
la gui-ta-re, lă gee tăr'.	the guitar.	re-con-qué-rir,* ruh kōn ka reer.	to conquer [again.
la ga-geu-re, lă gă zhür'.	the wager.	ma-ro-quin,* mă rŏ kĭn.	morocco-leather.
le gyp-se, luh zheeps'.	gypsum.	ty-pi-que, tee peek'.	typical.
Gui-zot, ba-gue, gee zo, băg'.	Guizot, ring.	pour-quoi, poor kweh.	why.

Régularité, tu agaças, la rougeole, vagabond, une guéridon, la guitare, la gageure, le gypse, Guizot, bague, hôpital, horloge, un joujou, le jujube, mon jardin, reconquérir, maroquin, typique, pourquoi.

---

* Reconquérir, maroquin, &c., will be spelled: ruh uh ruh, kuh ōn, kōn, ruhkōn, kuh a ka, ruhkōnka, ruh ee ruh reer, ruhkōnkareer; muh ă mă, ruh ŏ rŏ, mărŏ, kuh ĭn kĭn, mărŏkĭn; &c.

ă, as; ah, ăh, father; uh, ermine; ĕ or ', move; a, late; eh, met; ēh, there; ee, police; ŏ, nor; o, also; ō, no; ŭ, constitution; ēū, first; oo, too; ān, want; ĭn, Yānkee; ōn, don't; ūn, grunt; weh, wear; wah, water; g, go; zh, glazier.

THEORY.

EIGHTH LESSON. *Huitième leçon.*

CONSONANTS.

S.

41. s between two vowels has the sound of z in *zone*, and is called *zuh;* everywhere else it is pronounced as s in *so*, and is called *suh.*

TI.

42. The combination ti is pronounced *see* in cases when, in English, it sounds as sh in *she.*

Ex.—action, patient, pronounced *ăk see ōn, pă see ān.*

X.

43. x is, in French, pronounced in five different ways:—

1°. as gz, and is then called *gzuh.* 1st, At the beginning of words. 2d, In the particle ex followed by a vowel.
2°. as ks. 1st, Between two vowels. 2d, Before ca, co, cu, and qu. 3d, Before any consonant, *h* and *s* excepted. 4th, When final and sounded. It is then called *ksuh.*
3°. as k, before oe, oé, cè, and s; and is called *kuh.*
4°. as s in *so.* In *soixante* and its compounds and derivatives, in *Aix-les-Bains*, in *dix-sept*, and in *six* and *dix* used without a substantive. It then takes the name *suh.*

Obs.—The x of *dix* and *six* is silent before a *noun* or an *adjective* beginning with a consonant; but it takes the z sound before a vowel or a mute h, and is then called *zuh.*

5°. as z in *zone;* in *deuxième, sixième, sixain, dixième, dix-huit, dix-neuf;* also when final and carried to the next word beginning with a vowel or a mute h. It then assumes the name *zuh.* (See §§ 12, 13.)

PRACTICE.

EIGHTH EXERCISE. *Huitième exercice.*

Il moi-si-ra, *eel mweh zee ră.*	it will mould.	Ex-cès, lu-xe, *ak† seh, lŭks'.*	excess, luxury.
la dic-tion,* *lă deek see ōn.*	the diction.	e-xhi-bi-tion, *a gzee bee see ōn.*	exhibition.
un pa-tient,* *ŭn pă see ān.*	a patient.	soi-xan-te, *sweh sāut'.*	sixty.
Xi-mé-nés, *gzee ma nehs.*	Ximenes.	ex-cu-ses, *ak*t küz'.*	excuses.
e-xa-mi-nons, *a gză mee nōn.*	let us examine.	Fé-lix, o-nyx, *fa leeks, ŏ neeks.*	Felix, onyx.
e-xo-ti-que,* *a gzŏ teek'.*	exotic.	ex-cé-dant, *ak*t sa dān.*	exceeding.
ex-po-si-tion,* *aks*t po zee see ōn.*	exposure.	ex-su-dant, *ak*t sŭ dān.*	perspiring.

Il moisira, la diction, un patient, Ximénés, examinons, exotique, exposition, excès, luxe, exhibition, soixante, excuses, Félix, onyx, excédant, exsudant.

---

* Diction, patient, exotique, and exposition will be spelled: duh ee kuh deek, suh ee ōn seeōn, deekseeōn; puh ă pă, suh ee ān seean, păseean; a ksuh aks, puh o po, akspo, zuh ee zee, akspozee, suh ee ōn seeōn, akspozeeseeōn; a, gzuh ŏ gzŏ, agzŏ, tuh ee tee, agzŏtee, kuh uh kuh, agzŏteek'.

† The student will remember that, in the written pronunciation, the a, without any mark, *must invariably* be sounded as a in late, regardless of the letters which precede or follow it.

ă, as; ah, āh, father; uh, ermine; ĕ or ', move; a, late; eh, met; ēh, there; ee, police; ŏ, nor; o, also; ō, no; ŭ, constitution; ēu, first; oo, too; ān, want; īn, Yankee; ōn, don't; ūn, grunt; weh, wear; wah, water; g̃, go; zh, glazier.

THEORY.

NINTH LESSON. *Neuvième leçon.*

COMBINED CONSONANTS.

44. The combined or inseparable consonants are never separated in the syllabification of words. They are considered as one articulation, and pronounced accordingly in one explosion, or with one impulsion of the voice.

THE TWENTY-THREE GROUPS OF COMBINED CONSONANTS.

1. bl,*	as in	blur,	called bluh.	13. ph,	as in	phial,	called fuh.
2. br,	,,	brush,	,, bruh.	14. phl,	,,	phlegm,	,, fluh.
3. ch,	,,	machine,	,, shuh.	15. phr,	,,	phrase,	,, fruh.
4. chr,	,,	chromo,	,, kruh.	16. pl,	,,	plum,	,, pluh.
5. cl,	,,	club,	,, kluh.	17. pr,	,,	prussia,	,, pruh.
6. cr,	,,	crush,	,, kruh.	18. rh,	,,	rhumb,	,, ruh.
7. dr,	,,	drum,	,, druh.	19. th,	as t in tub,		,, tuh.
8. fl,	,,	flush,	,, fluh.	20. thl,	as tl in titling,		,, tluh.
9. fr,	,,	frush,	,, fruh.	21. thr,	as tr in trudge,		,, truh.
10. gl,	,,	glum,	,, gluh.	22. tr,	as tr in trudge,		,, truh.
11. gn,	as ng in singing,		,, gnuh.	23. vr,	as in chevron,		,, vruh.
12. gr,	as in grudge,		,, gruh.				

45. DOUBLE CONSONANTS.—When a consonant is doubled, the first is generally silent, but by no means useless, for it indicates that the syllable to which it belongs is short.

---

* The pronunciation of English words ending with **e** preceded by combined consonants is peculiar. The two final letters interchange places: the **e**, assuming what is known as the obscure **u** sound, is virtually intercalated between the two preceding consonants. Thus, **amiable, eagle, centre, waffle,** &c., are pronounced *amiabul, eagul, centur, wafful,* &c. This never happens in French. The two consonants adhere to each other as closely as at the beginning of words; and the two consonant sounds, squeezed into one single articulation, come out in one explosion of the voice. Thus, **aimable, aigle, centre, rafle,** &c., are regularly pronounced, *aimabl', aigl', centr', rafl',* &c. The strength of the voice resting upon the penult, the sounding breath expires upon the last consonant of the final syllable.

LETTERS.

PRACTICE.

NINTH EXERCISE. *Neuvième exercice.*

⁸Le chant,* ¹²blond, ¹⁵the singing, [flaxen.		
luh shāṅ, blōṅ.		
¹⁶un gros ⁹clou, ¹²a big nail.		
ūṅ gro kloo.		
¹la brû-lu-re, ¹⁰ ¹⁰ ⁴the burn.		
lă brü lür'.		
¹⁰u-ne flû-te, ¹⁰ ⁴a flute.		
ūn' flüt'.		
¹la gri-ma-ce, ⁷ ¹ ⁴the wry face.		
lă gree măs'.		
chro-no-mè-tre, chronometer.		
krŏ nŏ mehtr'.		
¹⁰u-ne ⁴phra-²se, ⁴a sentence.		
ūn' frähs'.		
⁵phlé-³bo-³to-⁷mie,* bleeding.		
fla bŏ tŏ mee.		
⁵phré-³no-³lo-⁷gie, phrenology.		
fra nŏ lŏ zhee.		

¹⁶Un ⁷pry-¹ta-⁵née, a prytaneum.		
ūṅ pree tă na.		
¹⁰u-ne ⁴drô-³le-⁴rie, ⁷a drollery.		
ūn' drōl' ree.		
⁸chro-¹ma-⁷ti-⁴que, chromatic.		
krŏ mă teek'.		
¹la ¹⁰fru-¹ga-⁷li-⁴té, the frugality.		
lă frü gă lee tă.		
⁵phlé-³bo-³lo-⁷gie, treatise on the [veins.		
fla bŏ lŏ zhee.		
⁶phleg-¹ma-⁷sie,* phlegmasia.		
flehg mă zee.		
⁵phé-³no-⁶mè-⁴ne, phenomenon.		
fa nŏ mehn'.		
⁵thé-²à-¹tral, theatrical.		
ta ăh träl.		
⁸chro-⁷ni-⁴que, chronicle.		
krŏ neek'.		

Le chant, blond, un gros clou, la brûlure, une flûte, la grimace, chronomètre, une phrase, phlébotomie, phrénologie, un prytanée, une drôlerie, chromatique, la frugalité, phlébologie, phlegmasie, phénomène, théâtral, chronique.

---

* Chant, phlébotomie, phlegmasie, &c., will be spelled: shuh āṅ shāṅ; fluh a fla, buh ŏ bŏ, flabŏ, tuh ŏ tŏ, flabŏtŏ, muh ee mee, flabŏtŏmee; fluh eh gub flehg, muh ă mă, flehgmă, zuh ee zee, flehgmăzee; &c.

ă, as; ah, äh, father; uh, ermine; ĕ or ', move; a, late; eh, met; ēh, there; ee, police; ŏ, nor; o, also; ō, no; ŭ, constitution; ēū, first; 'oo, too; āṅ, want; īṅ, Yankee; ōṅ, don't; ūṅ, grunt; weh, wear; wah, water; g̃, go; zh, glazier.

THEORY.

TENTH LESSON. *Dixième leçon.*

VOWEL LETTERS AND SOUNDS.

46. THE FIRST VOWEL-SOUND (*a* in **as**) is represented :

1°. By a without accent (except in the cases stated in the next lesson).

2°. By à. (Here the grave accent is used to distinguish words containing the same letters, but having a different meaning.)

3°. By ea. (This combination occurs after g. The e, which is here a mere orthographic letter, is used to indicate that the g retains its soft sound as z in *glazier*.)

4°. By â and eâ; but only in the terminations *âmes, âtes, ât, eâmes, eâtes, eât*, of the verbs of the first conjugation.*

5°. By ai before l liquid.†

6°. By ai before ll liquid, but only in *médaille, médailliste, médaillier, médaillon, bataillon;* in all the tenses of *travailler, détailler, ravitailler;* and in those of *falloir, valoir, faillir, saillir, jaillir,* and *tressaillir*, which contain the combination *aill*, also, in their derivatives.

7°. By the e of *emm* in the middle of words.

8°. By the e of *enn* in *s'ennuiter, solennel, hennir*, and in words of the same radical.

47. CONCERNING THE LETTER a. — When two a's occur at the beginning of words, only one is heard; as in **Aalen, Aar, Aarun, Aarbourg, Aarrhus, aavora**, which are pronounced *Alen, Ar, Arun, Arbourg,* &c. **Aaron** is pronounced *Aron* in poetry, but in prose the two *a*'s are felt.

In the middle of words the a's form two distinct syllables: **Baal, Isaac, Balaam,** &c., are pronounced *Ba-al, I-sa-ac, Ba-la-am.*

---

* The circumflex accent, which is in French, as it is in Latin, the sign of contraction, indicates the suppression of a letter, — *s* in the case above, *allasmes, allastes,* &c. In these terminations it does not alter the a sound in its quality, but only and slightly in its quantity, causing it to be a little longer.

† l liquid, it will be remembered, is pronounced as **y** in *yes*.

PRACTICE.

TENTH EXERCISE.   *Dixième exercice.*

¹²Nous dé-⁵tail-¹lons,*¹⁵ we retail. noo da tă yŏṅ.	¹⁶Un por-³tail,¹ a portal. ŭṅ pŏr tă yŏ.	
¹⁵on ra-¹vi-⁷tail-¹le,⁴ they provision. ōṅ ră vee tă yŏ.	¹Ba-¹al, ¹I-⁷sa-¹ac, Baal, Isaac. bă ăl, eo ză ăk.	
²que ³je ¹vail-¹le,⁴ that I may be [worth. kuh zhuh vă yŏ.	¹aa-³vo-¹ra, palm-trees. ă vŏ ră.	
¹⁰du ⁵bé-¹tail, some cattle. dŭ ba tă yŏ.	¹la ¹fem-¹me,*⁴ the woman. lă făm'.	
¹²vous ¹³man-geâ-¹tes,⁴ you did eat. voo mäṅ zhăt'.	⁸so-¹len-⁷ni-⁵té, solemnity. sŏ lă nee ta.	
¹⁰tu ⁵gé-⁷mi-¹ras, thou shalt bemoan. tŭ zha mee ră.	⁷il ¹hen-⁷ni-¹ra, it will neigh. eel ă nee ră.	
²le ⁷vi-¹trail, the stained glass. luh vee tră yŏ.	²le ¹bras, the arm. luh bră.	
¹²nous ¹⁵son-geâ-¹mes,⁴ we thought. noo sōṅ zhăm'.	⁷il ¹jail-¹lit,⁷ it springs. eel zhă yee.	

Nous détaillons, on ravitaille, que je vaille, du bétail, vous mangeâtes, tu gémiras, le vitrail, nous songeâmes, un portail, Baal, Isaac, aavora, la femme, solennité, il hennira, le bras, il jaillit.

---

* **Nous détaillons** will be spelled: nuh oo **noo**; duh a **da**, tuh ă **tă**, **dată**, yuh ōṅ **yōṅ**, **datăyōṅ**; noo **datăyōṅ**. La femme will be spelled: luh ă **lă**; fuh ă **fă**, muh uh **muh**, **făm'**; lă **făm'**; &c.

ă, as; ah, äh, father; uh, ermine; ĕ or ', move; a, late; eh, met; ēh, there; ee, police; ŏ, nor; o, also; ō, no; ŭ, constitution; ēu, first; oo, too; äṅ, want; īṅ, Yankee; ōṅ, don't; ūṅ, grunt; weh, wear; wah, water; ğ, go; zh, glazier; g̅ṅ, singing; ȳ, yes.

THEORY.

ELEVENTH LESSON. *Onzième leçon.*

VOWEL LETTERS AND SOUNDS (*continued*).

47. CONCERNING THE LETTER a. — When **a** is preceded or followed by **o**, it generally retains its proper sound; and the **o**, detached from it, forms a distinct syllable: **cacao, chaos, Pharaon, Laodicée, Laocoon, Bilbao, caoutchouc, aorte, aoûter, oasis, boa, Goa, Antigoa,** &c., are pronounced *ca-ca-o, cha-os, o-a-sis, bo-a,* &c.

a is silent in **taon, Saint-Laon, Août, aoûteron, Saône, toast, curaçao, aoriste, saoul, saouler**; pronounced *ton, Saint-Lon, oût, oûteron, Sône, tost, cuiraço, oriste, sou, sou-lé.* On the contrary, **o** is null in **faon, faonner, Laon, paon, paonne, panneau, Craon**; pronounced *fan, fanner, Lan, pan, panne, panneau, Cran.*

Mme. de Staël is pronounced *stahl* or *sta-ël:* either pronunciation is correct.

48. THE SECOND VOWEL-SOUND (as **a** in *father*) is represented by **â** and **eâ**, except, as we have seen in the preceding lesson, in the terminations of verbs, — *âmes, âtes, ât, eâmes, eâtes, eât.*

49. **a**, without accent, represents also the second vowel-sound.

1°. Before **s** and **z** final, except in verbs and in **bras**, *arm*.
2°. In the derivatives of words ending in **as** (few exceptions).
3°. Before **se, ze,** and **rr** (generally).
4°. In words borrowed from the Latin.
5°. In **ai** before **ll** liquid.
6°. Before **tion**.
7°. In the syllables **qua** and **gua** when the **u** is sounded as **oo** in *too*. (This rule will be fully explained further on.)

PRACTICE.

ELEVENTH EXERCISE.   *Onzième exercice.*

Bas, bas-se,	low, low (f.).	
bah, bahs'.		
nous ra-mas-sons,	we gather up.	
noo ră mah sōn.		
un va-se, ga-ze,	a vase, gauze.	
ŭn vahz', gahz'.		
la mu-rail-le,*	the wall.	
lă mŭ rah yĕ.		
la pail-le,*	the straw.	
lă pah yĕ.		
le re-pas, le gaz,	the meal, the [gas.	
luh ruh pah, luh gahz.		
ils sont las,	they are tired.	
eel sōn lah.		
las-si-tu-de,	fatigue.	
lah see tud'.		

Le da-mas,	the damask.	
luh dă mah.		
da-mas-sé,	damasked.	
dă mah sa.		
ras, ra-se, dé-gât,	close-shaved, [havoc.	
rah rahz', da gah.		
un pas, pas-ser,	a step, to pass.	
ŭn pah, pah sa.		
u-ne ba-tail-le,	a battle.	
ŭn' bă tah yĕ.		
la vo-ca-ti-on,	the vocation.	
lă vŏ kah see ōn.		
qua-dru-pè-de,	quadruped.	
koo ah drŭ pehd'.		
a-ve, pa-ter,	ave, pater.	
ah va, pah tehr.		

Bas, basse, nous ramassons, un vase, gaze, la muraille, la paille, le repas, le gaz, ils sont las, lassitude, le damas, damassé, ras, rase, dégât, un pas, passer, une bataille, la vocation, quadrupède, ave, pater.

---

* Muraille, paille, &c., will be spelled: muh ŭ mŭ, ruh ah rah, mŭrah, ȳuh uh ȳuh, mŭrahȳĕ; puh ah pah, ȳuh uh yuh, pahȳĕ; &c.

ă, as; ah, äh, father; uh, ermine; ŏ or ', move; a, late; eh, met; eh, there; ee, police; ŏ, nor; o, also; ō, no; ŭ, constitŭtion; eū, first; oo, too; añ, want; iñ, Yankee; oñ, don't; ūñ, grunt; weh, wear; wah, water; g̃, go; zh, glazier; g̃ñ, singing; ȳ, yes.

THEORY.

TWELFTH LESSON. *Douzième leçon.*

VOWEL LETTERS AND SOUNDS (*continued*).

50. **a** without accent is also sounded as **a** in *father* in the following words and those of the same radical: **accabler, gare! bah! occasion, chalet, ah! flamme, rare, tasse, échasse, Jeanne, rafle, miracle, jaser, calfat, allah! classe, casser, sabre, fable, jadis, lazzi, gazouiller, racler, lacer, grasseyer,** and a few others.

51. THE THIRD VOWEL-SOUND, which is identical with the sound of **e** in *ermine*, is represented by **e**, without accent, in monosyllabic words, and in syllables not final, containing no other vowel-letter than that **e**, and in *gue* and *que*.

This rich and well-characterized sound is also represented by the following combinations: —

1°. **eu, eue, œu,** but only before **b, f, l, il** liquid, **n** not final, **p, r,** and **v**.

2°. **œi, uei,** before l liquid.

OBS. — But **eu** initial, whether followed or not by any of the consonants enumerated above, always represents the 11th sound (as i in *first*).

52. When the unaccented **e** is the only vowel-letter of two or three successive syllables respectively, occurring at the beginning of a word, as in **recevoir, redevenir,** &c., the sound of one or two of those e's is dropped, at the option of the speaker, so as to obtain rapidity and greater ease and smoothness in the pronunciation.

OBS. — This sound (**e** as in *ermine*) is the *only vowel-sound* that is occasionally SLIGHTED in French. In conversation, that unaccented **e** is invariably silent, whenever the consonant before it can be pronounced either with the vowel preceding that consonant, or with the vowel beginning the syllable or word which immediately follows the **e**; precisely as, in English, in **intimately, pure affection**; pronounced *intimatly, pur affection.*

PRACTICE.

TWELFTH EXERCISE.   *Douzième exercice.*

² ² ² ⁴ [alone. Le veuf, seu-le, the widower, luh vuhf, suhl'.	¹² ⁴ ² ⁴ 15 [again. Nous re-de-ve-nons, we become noo r' duhv' nōn.
¹ ² ² la peur, l'œuf,* the fear, the egg. lă puhr, luhf.	² ¹² ² l'œil, dou-leur, the eye, grief. luhyă, doo luhr.
² ⁴ ² ⁴ neu-ve, l'heu-re, new, the hour. nuhv', luhr'.	16 11 un nœud, a knot. ūn neū.
² 11 11 ² ⁴ [Europe. le vœu, l'Eu-ro-pe, the vow, luh veū, leū rŏp'.	16 ² un bœuf, an ox. ūn buhf.
¹ ² 11 ma-lheu-reux,† unfortunate. mă luh reū.	¹ ² l'ac-cueil, the greeting. lă kuhyă.
¹ 1 ² l'a-ma-teur, the amateur. lă mă tuhr.	² ² 11 l'or-gueil-leux, § the proud one. lŏr ḡuh yeū.
² 1 ⁴ l'œil-la-de, ‡ the glance. luh yăd'.	10 1 ² 1 tu ac-cueil-las, thou welcomedst. tū ă kuh yă.

Le veuf, seule, la peur, l'œuf, neuve, l'heure, le vœu, l'Europe, malheureux, l'amateur, l'œillade, nous redevenons, l'œil, douleur, un nœud, un bœuf, l'accueil, l'orgueilleux, tu accueillas.

---

* The apostrophe (') is used in French to indicate the elision of a vowel. It does not affect, in the least, the sound of the consonant which precedes it, nor of the vowel which follows.

† **Malheureux** is etymologically divided thus: mal-heu-reux; but its pronunciation requires the division given in the exercise above.

‡ L'œillade, &c., will be spelled: luh uh luh, yuh ă yă, luhyă, duh uh duh, luhyădĕ.

§ L'orgueilleux is also pronounced lŏr ḡa yeū.

ă, as; ah, äh, father; uh, ermine; ĕ or ', move; a, late; eh, met; ēh, there; ee, police; ŏ, nor; o, also; ō, no; ŭ, constitution; eū, first; oo, too; ān, want; īn, Yankee; ōn, don't; ūn, grunt; weh, wear; wah, water; ḡ, go; zh, glazier; ḡn, singing; y, yes.

THEORY.

THIRTEENTH LESSON. *Treizième leçon.*

VOWEL LETTERS AND SOUNDS (*continued*).

53. In **ress** at the beginning of words, the **e** is sounded as in **e***rmine, ressource, ressembler, ressort,* &c. But in **ressui, ressuciter, ressuyer,** the first **e** has the value of **a** in *late*.

54. In **dessus, dessous, cheptel,** the **e** sounds as in **e***rmine*.

55. FOURTH VOWEL-SOUND. — The semi-mute **e** (as in *move*) represents an obscure sound, or rather an emission of breath hardly audible, — a mere vanishing of the voice. It really represents a want of sound in the escaping breath, and not a distinct vowel-sound.

56. The semi-mute **e** is not exclusively French: it exists also in a number of English words. For instance, in **basement, ceaseless, enticement, immediately, move, zone, take, bore,** &c., the *nearly silent* **e** is precisely similar to the semi-mute **e** of the French, which is indistinct, feeble, and the faintest of our vowel-sounds.

57. **e** not initial, and unaccented, of course, is semi-mute:
1°. When final and preceded by a consonant (in words of more than one syllable).
2°. Before a single consonant not final, **x** excepted.
3°. Before two consonants, the second being l or r.
4°. In **es** at the end of words of more than one syllable.
5°. In **ent,** termination of the third person plural of verbs.

OBS. — The semi-mute **e** forms naturally semi-mute syllables.

58. A semi-mute syllable generally lengthens the sound of the syllable preceding it.

59. **e** final preceded by a vowel is altogether silent, but not useless:
1°. It lengthens the sound of the preceding vowel.
2°. It is generally the distinctive mark of the feminine gender.

LETTERS. 31

PRACTICE.

THIRTEENTH EXERCISE. *Treizième leçon.*

La re-te-nue, là r' tuh nü.	the reserve.	Ils se re-voient, eel suh r' vweh.	[other again. they see each
le sé-ne-vé, luh sa n' va.	the charlock.	il par-le,* eel pärl'.	he speaks.
le ve-nin, luh v' nin.	the venom.	ils par-lent, eel pärl'.	they speak.
ils dé-ve-lop-pent, eel da v' lŏp'.	they unfold.	for-fan-te-rie, fŏr fän t' ree.	bragging.
ils se dé-vouent, eel suh da voo.	they devote [themselves.	dé-con-ve-nue, da kōn v' nü.	discomfiture.
ils mè-nent, eel mehn'.	they lead.	to-ni-que, to neek.	tonic.
un se-quin, ŭn s' kin.	a sequin.	quin-ze, kinz'.	fifteen.
un re-mè-de, ŭn r' mehd'.	a remedy.	l'a-na-to-mie, lä nä tŏ mee.	the anatomy.

La retenue, le séneve, le venin, ils développent, ils se dévouent, ils mènent, un sequin, un remède, ils se revoient, il parle, ils parlent, forfanterie, déconvenue, tonique, quinze, l'anatomie.

---

* The e of the termination *ent* of the third person plural of verbs was formerly sounded. Now, without being sounded, it borrows however from the consonants *nt* which follow it a value in quantity which it has not in the singular; and this quantitative difference between the singular and plural should always be felt.

ă, as; ah, âh, father; uh, ermine; ĕ or ', move; a, late; eh, met; ēh, there; ee, police; ŏ, nor; o, also; ō, no; ŭ, constitution; ēū, first; oo, too; a̅n̅, want; ī n̅, Yankee; ō n̅, don't; ū n̅, grunt; weh, wear; wah, water; ḡ, go; zh, glazier; ḡn, singing; ȳ, yes.

THEORY.

FOURTEENTH LESSON. *Quatorzième leçon.*

VOWEL LETTERS AND SOUNDS (*continued*).

60. In poetry, and particularly in singing, the **e**, which in prose would be semi-mute or altogether silent, is generally fully sounded.

61. **e**, without accent, is therefore sounded with different degrees of force and distinctness, according to place and circumstances.

In polysyllabic words, the medial **e** is either sounded distinctly, as in *comprenons,* or slighted in its pronunciation, as in **maintenant**; and very often, as we have already seen, its sound is dropped altogether, its function being simply to give a full sound to the preceding consonant. We generally drop the **e** sound whenever it is possible to do so. For instance, it is easier to pronounce **soutenir, maintenant, convenable, bonnement**, without the **e** sound, — thus: *soutnir, maintnant, convnable, bonniment;* consequently to drop the **e** sound in such words is correct. On the other hand, it is easier to give the medial **e** its full sound (as in ermine) when it is preceded by combined consonants, or some soft or liquid sounds, such as are represented by **r, l, s**; or when a semi-mute syllable whose **e** sound is dropped, immediately precedes it, as in *Charlemagne, considérablement, comprenons, redemandons,* &c.: therefore, in this case, the rule is to pronounce the **e** distinctly.*

---

* Obs. — When the semi-mute **e** is not preceded by a double consonant (rr excepted), it lengthens the syllable before it; and if that syllable is already a long one by its nature, such as those formed by nasal vowels or diphthongs, its position before the semi-mute **e** makes it, necessarily, still longer.

PRACTICE.

FOURTEENTH EXERCISE. *Quatorzième exercice.*

Le vi-gne-ron, l' veegn' ron.	the vine-dresser.	La fil-le, ci-guë,† lă feey', see gü	the girl, hem-[lock.
u-ne li-gne, ŭn' leegn'.	a line.	la froi-du-re, lă frweh dür'.	the coldness.
la cam-pa-gne, lă kān pagn'.	the country.	phi-lo-so-phie, fee lo zŏ fee.	philosophy.
la na-ï-ve-té,* lă nă eev' ta.	the artlessness.	ils meu-blent, eel muh bl'.	they furnish.
il tra-vail-le, eel tră văyĕ.	he works.	il meu-ble, eel muh bl'.	he furnishes.
ils tra-vail-lent, eel tră văyĕ.	they work.	le peu-ple, l' puh pl'.	the people.

Le vigneron, une ligne, la campagne, la naïveté, il travaille, ils travaillent, la fille, ciguë, la froidure, philosophie, ils meublent, il meuble, le peuple.

---

* The diæresis (¨), *diérèse*, or *tréma*, is used over e, i, and u (ë, ï, ü) to indicate that these vowels are not combined with the preceding one, but form a distinct syllable, and should be pronounced separately, retaining, of course, their proper sound.

† We have seen (page 18) that in gu followed by e, i, or y, the u is an orthographic letter, and as such silent; but that rule has the following exception: viz., when e is added to form the feminine of an adjective ending in the masculine in gu, that addition of e does not cause the u — which is, naturally, fully sounded in the masculine — to become silent in the feminine, inasmuch as it is not the u, but the e, which is the orthographic letter in this case. The diæresis, then, over the ë, indicates that the latter does not affect the regular pronunciation of the u.

ă, as; ah, âh, father; uh, ermine; ĕ or ', move; a, late; eh, met; ĕh, there; ee, police; ŏ nor; o, also; ō, no; ŭ, constitution; eu, first; oo, too; an, want; in, Yankee; on, don't; un, grunt; weh, wear; wah, water; g, go; zh, glazier; gn, singing; y, yes.

THEORY.

FIFTEENTH LESSON. *Quinzième leçon.*

VOWEL LETTERS AND SOUNDS (*continued*).

62. In the termination **ent** of the third person plural of verbs, the **e** is silent together with **nt**, mark of the plural; but, according to rule, **nt** lengthens the preceding syllable: hence, il parle and ils parlent, il prie and ils prient, differ, but only in the quantity, or duration of sound, the plural being longer than the singular.

63. It must be remembered that the termination **ent** is silent in the *third person* PLURAL *of verbs only:* everywhere else the **e** of that termination coalesces with the **n**, forming a nasal sound which is fully and distinctly pronounced. The following list will sufficiently illustrate this rule:—

Ils affluent, eel ză flu.	they abound.	Un affluent, a tributary stream. ūn nă flu ăn.	
ils content, eel kōnt'.	they relate.	il est content, he is contented. eel eh kōn tăn.	
ils convergent, eel kōn vehrzh'.	they converge.	convergent (adj.), convergent. kōn vehr zhăn.	
ils envient, eel zăn vee.	they envy.	il en vient, he comes thence. eel ăn vee īn.	
ils expédient, eel zaks pa dee.	they despatch.	un expédient, an expedient. ūn naks pa dee ăn.	
ils excellent, eel zaks ehl'.	they excel.	c'est excellent, that is excellent. seh taks a lăn.	
ils précèdent, eel pra-sehd'.	they precede.	un précédent, a precedent. ūn pra sa dăn.	

PRACTICE.

FIFTEENTH EXERCISE.   *Quinzième exercice.*

Ils adhèrent, they adhere. eel ză dehr'.	Un adhérent, an adherent. ūn nă da rāū.
ils convient, they invite. eel kōn vee.	il convient, it is suitable. eel kōn vee īn.
ils diffèrent, they defer. eel def fehr'.	c'est différent, it is different. seh dee fa rāū.
ils équivalent, they are equiva-[lent. eel za kee văl.	l'équivalent, the equivalent. la kee vă lāū.
ils négligent, they neglect. eel na gleezh'.	un négligent, a neglectful one. ūn na glee zhāū.
ils président, they preside. eel pra zeed.	le président, the president. l' pra zee dāū.
ils résident, they reside. eel ra zeed'.	un résident, a resident. ūn ra zee dāū.

NOTE. — In regard to quantity, one thing should be borne in mind ; viz., that syllables are not measured according to the *accidental* slowness or rapidity of their pronunciation, but relatively to the immutable proportions which make them short or long. Thus, of two persons, one may excessively lengthen his words, the other may hurry and sputter, and still both may duly and equally attend to the quantity ; for, although the sputterer may have pronounced a long syllable quicker than his companion a short one, neither the one nor the other may fail to make their syllables short or long as they should be, with this difference only, that one of them articulates his syllables in one fourth or fifth of the time which the other requires.

ă, as ; ah, âh, father ; uh, ermine ; ŏ or ', move ; a, late ; eh, met ; ēh, there ; ee, police ; ŏ, nor ; o, also ; ō, no ; ŭ, constitution ; ēū, first ; oo, too ; āū, want ; īn, Yankee ; ōū, don't ; ūū, grunt ; weh, **w**ear ; wah, **w**ater ; ḡ, go ; zh, glazier ; ḡn, singing ; ȳ, yes.

THEORY.

SIXTEENTH LESSON. *Seizième leçon.*

VOWEL LETTERS AND SOUNDS (*continued*).

64. When several monosyllabic words or syllables whose vowel-sound is represented by the unaccented e follow each other in uninterrupted succession, we drop the e sound of as many of these syllables as is necessary to obtain rapidity of utterance and smoothness and ease in pronunciation; and thus the monotony which would result from the repetition of the same sound in successive syllables is avoided.

OBS. — Unsuccessful attempts have been made to establish rules which would indicate with certainty which of these successive syllables should suppress the e sound, and which retain it in full (as in ermine). Good elocutionists disregard (with reason) such *definite* rules; and the general principle which governs our best speakers is this: —

65. The e sound should be dropped whenever the articulation accompanying the vowel e can be pronounced without it.

66. It is, however, a pretty general custom, in conversation, to drop the e sound of every alternate syllable; the first, third, fifth, &c., only being sounded.

OBS. — But this is not a binding rule. The speaker may, as it has already been said, slur or omit altogether the e sound whenever rapidity, convenience, euphony, or even his own taste require it. The syllable **que** is, of all, the one more frequently pronounced distinctly.

67. In poetry the syllable containing the unaccented e is generally reckoned as one foot of the verse, and therefore fully sounded.

68. The combination **ai** of **faire**, *to make*, and derivatives, is irregularly pronounced as e in her, in the tenses of that verb having two sonorous syllables, and that sound is subjected to the foregoing rules.

PRACTICE

SIXTEENTH EXERCISE.   *Seizième exercice.*

<small>3 4   3   4</small>
Je le don-ne,   I give it.
<small>zhuh l'   dŏn'.</small>

<small>3   4 3   4   3   4 2</small>
Je ne le don-ne pas,   I do not give it.
<small>zhuh n' luh dŏn'   pah.</small>

<small>3   4 3 4 3   4</small>
Que je te le don-ne,   That I may give it to thee.
<small>kuh zh'tuh l'   dŏn'.</small>

<small>3   4 3 4   3   3   4 2</small>
Que je ne te le don-ne pas,   That I may not give it to thee.
<small>kuh zh' nuh t' luh dŏn' pah.</small>

<small>1   4   3 4. 3   4 3   3   9   4 2</small>   [it to myself.
Par-ce que je ne me le pro-po-se pas, Because I do not propose
<small>pārs' kuh zh' nuh m'luh prŏ poz' pah.</small>

<small>3 4   3   4 3   4 3 7   4 2</small>   [to thee.
De ce que je ne te le don-ne pas,   Because I do not give it
<small>duh s' kuh zh' nuh t' luh dŏn pah.</small>

<small>3 4   3   4 3   4 3   4   13   4 2</small>   [of thee.
De ce que je ne te le de-man-de pas, Because I do not ask it
<small>duh s' kuh zh' nuh t' luh d' mānd' pah.</small>

<small>3   4 3   4 3   4 3 4   3 13   4 2</small>   [again from thee.
De ce que je ne te le re-de-man-de pas, Because I do not ask it
<small>duh s' kuh zh' nuh t' luh r' duh mānd' pah.</small>

<small>12   3   15   7   3   6</small>
Nous fai-sons, ils fai-saient,   We do, they were doing.
<small>noo fuh zōn, eel fuh zeh.</small>

<small>7 14 3 13   7 14 3   13   4</small>
Bien fai-sant, bien-fai-san-ce,   Benevolent, benevolence.
<small>bee īn fuh zān, bee īn fuh zāns'.</small>

ă, as; ah, âh, father; uh, ermine; ĕ or ', move; a, late; eh, met; ōh, there; ee, police; ŏ, nor; o, also; ō, no; ŭ, constitution; ēū, first; oo, too; āṉ, want; īṉ, Yankee; ōṉ, don't; ūṉ, grunt; weh, wear; wah, water; ḡ, go; zh, glazier; ḡṉ, singing; ȳ, yes.

THEORY.

SEVENTEENTH LESSON. *Dix-septième leçon.*

VOWEL LETTERS AND SOUNDS (*continued*).

69. FIFTH VOWEL-SOUND. — The acute **é**, which has the greatest intensity of all the e's, is always short, and neatly pronounced. Our **é** is the short **e** of the Latin: **élégant, elegans; élément, elementum.** It represents the fifth sound of our scale.

70. When the English words **late, gate, paper,** are uttered with brevity, their **a** sound is equivalent to that of the French **é**.

71. This acute sound (**a** in late) is also represented by the following combinations of letters, but only in the positions and circumstances herein specified: —

1°. **œ** initial, before a consonant.
2°. **er, ez,** and **ée,** final.
3°. **ai, eai, aie,** final, but in verbs only.
4°. **et** conjunction (whose **t** is always silent).
5°. **ai** in *je sais, tu sais, il sait, gai, fantaisie, fraisil, saisir, fainéant, quai, plaisir,* and a few other words, given in subsequent lessons.

72. **e** without accent is also sounded as **a** in *late* (fifth vowel-sound).

1°. Before a doubled consonant not immediately followed by another unaccented **e**.
2°. In the prefix **ex**, and in words borrowed from the Latin and Italian languages.
3°. Before **d** final, except in proper names.
4°. In **les, des, ces, mes, tes, ses.**
5°. In **es** initial, except when **es** has the force of a preposition.

OBS. — The acute **é** *never* coalesces with the following vowel, but it may form a diphthongal syllable with the vowel preceding it.

PRACTICE.

SEVENTEENTH EXERCISE. *Dix-septième exercice.*

Œ-cu-mé-ni-que,* a kü ma neek'.	œcumenical.	Se ré-cré-er, s' ra kra a.	to divert one's self.
vous me-na-cez, voo m' nă sa.	you threaten.	les pieds,† la pee a.	the feet.
de-vi-ner, d' vee na.	to guess.	que j'aie, kuh zha.	that I may have.
le nez, je se-rai, l' na, zhuh s' ra.	[shall be. the nose, I	es pè·ces, as pehs'.	species.
je ju-geai, zhuh zhü zha.	I judged.	es-car-bou-cle, as kăr bookl'.	carbuncle.
va sur le quai, vă sür luh ka.	[wharf. go upon the	il s'as-sied, eel să see a.	he sits down.
je-tez le frai-sil, zh' ta l' fra zee.	[the coal-dross. throw away	es-pé-rer, as pa ra.	to hope.
ec-ce ho-mo, ak sa ō mō.	ecce homo.	je par-le-rai, zh' păr luh ra.	I shall speak.

Œcuménique, vous menacez, deviner, le nez, je serai, je jugeai, va sur le quai, jetez le fraisil, ecce homo, se récréer, les pieds, que j'aie, espèces, escarboucle, il s'assied, espérer, je parlerai.

---

* The letter i has the most acute sound of all the vowels; then comes the é; next, the è, which varies most of all; the ê, which is the broadest of the e's; and, finally, ă, which is the most open and the longest of all the vowel-sounds.

† s, mark of the plural, lengthens (slightly) the last sonorous sound of the word.

ă, as; ah, âh, father; uh, ermine; ŏ or ', move; a, late; eh, met; ēh, there; ee, police; ŏ, nor; o, also; ō, no; ŭ, constitution; eū, first; oo, too; a͞n, want; i͞n, Yankee; o͞n, don't; u͞n, grunt; weh, wear; wah, water; ḡ, go; zh, glazier; ḡn, singing; ȳ, yes.

THEORY.

EIGHTEENTH LESSON. *Dix-huitième leçon.*

VOWEL LETTERS AND SOUNDS (*continued*).

73. CONCERNING THE LETTER é. — At the beginning of many words, the acute accent is essentially euphonic. It there supplies the place of the letter s which is now omitted, — école, écrit, écaille, &c., were formerly written *eschole, escript, escaille*, &c., from the Latin *schola, scriptum, squamma*, &c.

74. In many other words which have retained the s, the initial unaccented e is sounded é (see § 72, 5°): thus, escabeau, espérer, &c., are pronounced *éscabeau, éspérer*, &c.

75. But e is (regularly) sounded (as in met) when es initial has the force of a preposition indicating separation, and represents the ex of the Latin: escompter, *ex-completare*, estime, *existimatio*, &c., are pronounced *èscompter, èstimer*, &c.

OBS. — When e without accent is said to be pronounced like the acute é, its sound is never so close nor brief, however, as that of é. On the other hand, it is, of course, never so open as that of the grave è.

76. er final has generally the value of é; but when the r is carried to the next word, which is the case in poetry, in serious reading, and in the elevated or noble style, the e sound, then affected by the sounded r, is not quite so close as that of é.

77. The termination ége is invariably pronounced *ège*. Here the acute accent is retained by reason of etymology (by the Academy); but many writers, in conformity with the pronunciation, use, very rationally, the grave accent, — an orthography which will ultimately prevail.

PRACTICE.

EIGHTEENTH EXERCISE. *Dix-huitième exercice.*

⁵ ¹ ¹² L'es-ca-dron, lasĕ kă drōn.	the squadron.	⁵ ⁵ ⁸ ⁷ ⁵ Les es-tro-piés, la zasĕ trŏ pee a.	the crippled.
⁵ ¹ ¹ ⁵ es-ca-la-der, asĕ kă lă da.	to climb over.	⁷ ⁸ ⁶ ⁴ il pro-té-ge, eel prŏ tehzh'.	he protects.
⁵ ² ⁴ l'es-pa-ce, lasĕ pahs'.	the space.	³ ⁸ ⁶ ⁴ le col-lé-ge, luh kŏ lehzh'.	the college.
⁵ ⁸ ¹ l'es-to-mac, lasĕ tŏ mă.	the stomach.	¹⁶ ⁵ ⁹ un cre-do, ūn kra do.	a creed.
¹⁶ ⁵ ⁷ ⁶ ⁴ un es-piè-gle,* ūn nasĕ pee ehḡl'.	a frolicsome one.	⁷ ⁵ ⁶ ² vi-ce ver-sâ, vee sa vehr sah.	vice versa.

* The French ear has a strong partiality for the smooth and pleasant vowel-sounds. This is manifested by the readiness with which the voice rests upon those sounds. Hence, as we have already seen, the strongly articulated consonant sounds after which a pause, however short, may be made, are generally dropped; because the voice, in sympathy with the ear, feels an instinctive repugnance to stop, rest, or even make the slightest pause upon what is rough, abrupt, angular, and seek to linger upon what is smooth and soft. But when there is no stoppage, no pause, or rest, to be made, — as, for example, between words which, from their intimate connection in sense, cannot be disjoined in reading, even by the smallest appreciable break in the flow of the voice; and when, moreover, by dropping the final consonant-sound of the first word, a hiatus or gap in the voice would result, as in the case of the second word beginning with a vowel, an occurrence which is very frequent in French, — then, in order to avoid the hiatus or meeting of two vowel-sounds, the final consonant of the first word, which in other circumstances would be silent, is restored to its full value as an articulation, and takes its place, as a sounded consonant, at the beginning of the second word. Thus, **un ami, les aveux**, are pronounced *un nami, les zaveux*.

ă, as; ah, āh, father; uh, ermine; ĕ or ', move; a, late; eh, met; ēh, there; ee, police; ŏ, nor; o, also; ō, no; ŭ, constitution; eū, first; oo, too; aṉ, want; īṉ, Yankee; ōṉ, don't; ūṉ, grunt; weh, wear; wah, water; ḡ, go; zh, glazier; ḡṉ, singing; ȳ, yes.

THEORY.

NINETEENTH LESSON. *Dix-neuvième leçon.*

VOWEL LETTERS AND SOUNDS (*continued*).

78. SIXTH VOWEL-SOUND. — The grave è has a broad, open sound, which the e of *met* would exactly represent, if the English sound were not so abrupt and snapping. The French sound is, according to circumstances, more or less open, varying between that of e in *met* and that of e in *there*, and is the sixth in our scale.

79. The following combinations represent also the sixth vowel-sound: —

1°. ei, ay, ey, everywhere.
2°. ai, aie, eai, except when final in verbs. (See § 71, 3°.)
3°. ê, eî, aî, represent the long sound (e in *there*).
4°. ei in *reine* has also the same long sound.

80. e without accent is also sounded as in *met*, when it is followed by a consonant in the same syllable, except m, n, x, and provided the consonant be not doubled, in which latter case e is sounded as a in *late*.

81. But when a doubled consonant preceded by e is also followed by another unaccented e, the first e assumes the sound of è (as in *met*). (See § 72, 1°.)

82. When the combination er is not final, it is *always* pronounced as *ere* in English.

83. In every language there is, in each word *pronounced separately*, one syllable uttered with a peculiar force — with a greater stress of the voice — than the others. In French that accented syllable is always the *last sonorous syllable* of the word.

LETTERS. 43

PRACTICE.

NINETEENTH EXERCISE. *Dix-neuvième exercice.*

La vei-ne, lă vehn'.	the vein.	Ge-ler, il-gè-le, zh' la, eel zhehl'.	to freeze, it [freezes.
Fon-te-nay, fōnt' neh.	Fontenay.	la rei-ne, lă rĕhn'.	the queen.
Guer-ne-sey, ḡehr nuh zeh.	Guernsey.	l'ap-pel, lă pehl.	the roll-call.
la se-mai-ne, lă s' mehn'.	the week.	mer-ci, mehr see.	thank you.
tu sou-la-geais, tü soo lă zheh.	thou didst re-[lieve.	les pin-cet-tes, la pīn seht'.	the tongs.
la ton-nel-le, lă tŏ nehl'.	the arbor.	la cer-vel-le, lă sehr vehl'.	the brain.
pa-reil-le, pă rehy'.	similar.	l'en-ne-mi,* lehn' mee.	the enemy.
mer-veil-leu-s'e, mehr veh yēūz'.	wonderful.	il a per-ce-vait, eel ă pehr suh veh.	he perceived.

La veine, Fontenay, Guernesey, la semaine, tu soulageais, la tonnelle, pareille, merveilleuse, geler, il gèle, la reine, l'appel, merci, les pincettes, la cervelle, l'ennemi, il apercevait.

---

* When a consonant is doubled, the first is silent; hence, when **m** or **n** is doubled, the first, being silent, does not form a nasal sound with the preceding vowel, which retains its proper sound. e before *nne* is accordingly pronounced as e in *met*. (See § 81.)

ă, as; ah, āh, father; uh, ermine; ĕ or ', move; a, late; eh, met; ēh, there; ee, police; ŏ, nor; o, also; ō, no; ŭ, constitution; ēū, first; oo, too; ān, want; īn, Yankee; ōn, don't; ūn, grunt; weh, **wear**; wah, **water**; ḡ, go; zh, glazier; ḡn, singing; ȳ, **y**és.

THEORY.

TWENTIETH LESSON. *Vingtième leçon.*

VOWEL LETTERS AND SOUNDS (*continued*).

84. PERMUTATIONS OF ACCENTS AND SOUNDS. — We have seen, by what precedes, that Accents are not all written. We shall see now, in what follows, that Written accents are not all pronounced; also that One sound may at times permute with another, and *vice versa.*

85. The **e**, accented or not, is, in many cases, affected by the character of the following syllable. When that syllable is a grave or a long one (such as those preceding a semi-mute syllable, and those formed of a diphthong or of a nasal vowel), the **e**, with or without accent, is generally pronounced with a broader, more open sound, not because of any established or arbitrary rules, but because it is a natural tendency to do so; and this is done by everybody, not only without effort, but without thought. Thus: **altérable, marécage, présence, connétable, épuiser, régence, répondu, désenfler, &c.**, are pronounced nearly as if they were written, *altèrable, marècage, prèsence, connètable, èpuiser, règence, &c.*

86. The letter **r** affects in the same manner the **e** of the preceding syllable, whether that **e** be accented or not; thus, **espérance, dégénérer, modération, persévérance, tempérer, suggérer, délibération, digérer, confédérés, &c.**, are pronounced nearly as if written, *espèrance, dégénèrer, modèration, persévèrance, &c.*

87. But the reverse takes place when **e**, with or without accent, is followed by a short or a close syllable (one that terminates with a consonant sound). Here the natural tendency is to the close, or acute **é**: thus, **interdiction, enregistrer, prêter, invectiver, &c.**, are very nearly pronounced *intérdiction, enrégistrer, préter, invéctiver, &c.*, as if they had the acute accent.

PRACTICE.

TWENTIETH EXERCISE. *Vingtième exercice.*

Con-naî-tre, kŏ nēhtr'.	to know.	La bê-ti-se,* lă ba teez'.	the silliness.
les reî-tres, la rēhtr',	the reiters.	il est tê-tu, eel eh ta tŭ.	he is stubborn.
tu l'in-ter-ro-geas, tŭ lĭn ta rŏ zhă.	[question him. thou didst	la mon-naie, lă mŏ neh.	the small change.
per-fec-ti-bi-li-té, pehr fehk tee bee lee ta.	[ness. improvable-	le so-leil, l' sŏ lehy.	the sun.
un mi-li-tai-re, ŭn mee lee tehr'.	a military man.	le ton-ner-re, l' tŏ nehr'.	the thunder.

Connaître, les reîtres, tu l'interrogeas, perfectibilité, un militaire, la bêtise, il est têtu, la monnaie, le soleil, le tonnerre.

---

* The tendency in French is more towards the acute than the grave sounds. This is particularly the case in Paris, while in some parts of the provinces they still adhere preferably to the grave and broad sounds. Thus, aide, aise, mêle, laisse, bête, &c., are pronounced, regularly, *éde, èse, mêle, lèsse, bète,* &c.; but aider, aisément, mêler, laissé, bêtise, &c., are pronounced *éder, ésément, méler, léssé, bétise.*

This tendency is well illustrated by the adopted pronunciation of some words, mostly proper names, whose unaccented e receives the full force of the acute é; such as **Fénelon**, which Voltaire wrote *Fénélon*, with two acute accents; **Richelieu, Perefixe**, which Michelet writes *Péréfixe*, with two acute é's, according to its pronunciation, and in spite of the authority of Perefixe himself; **refroidir, secrétaire, dangereux, aqueduc, degré**, the latter written *dégré* by Lafontaine, &c., and which are pronounced *Fénélon, Richélieu, Péréfixe, réfroidir, sécrétaire* or *sécretaire, dangéreux* (from danger), *aquéduc, dégré,* &c.

ă, as; ah, ăh, father; uh, ermine; ĕ or ', move; a, late; eh, met; ēh, there; ee, police; ŏ, nor; o, also; ō, no; ŭ, constitution; eū, first; oo, too; a̅n, want; ĭ̅n, Yankee; o̅n, don't; ŭ̅n, grunt; weh, wear; wah, water; ḡ, go; zh, glazier; ḡn, singing; ȳ, yes.

THEORY.

TWENTY-FIRST LESSON. *Vingt-et-unième leçon.*

VOWEL LETTERS AND SOUNDS (*continued*).

88. SEVENTH VOWEL-SOUND. — When i is not combined or does not coalesce with other letters, it is, *without exception*, sounded as i in *police*. Of all our vowels, i has the closest and most slender sound.

89. When i is followed by **m** or **n** in the same syllable, it generally coalesces with those consonants, and forms a nasal sound (14th).

90. But i followed by **m** or **n** retains its natural sound in words taken from foreign languages; also in **inn, imm,** at the beginning of words.

91. The unaccented **e** final following i does not alter the quality of the i sound, but slightly lengthens it, the **e** itself remaining silent.

92. The circumflex accent does not affect the sound of i.

93. When two i's follow each other, both are pronounced: the first being spoken very distinctly and somewhat dwelt upon; the second, which forms a diphthong with the following letters, rapidly and smoothly, and with a liquidity resembling that of il (in spelling, the second i sound is called *yuh*).

94. i is silent in **douairière, moignon, encoignure, oignon, poignée, poignet, poignard, Montaigne,** which are pronounced, *douarière, mognon, encognure, ognon, pognée, pognet, pognard, Montagne.**

95. CONCERNING THE LETTER **y.** — As its name (i grec) indicates, **y** is a Greek letter. It has, in sound and quantity, the value of one i.

96. But when, in the body of a word, it is preceded by a vowel, which occurs only in words purely French, it has the full force and value of two i's, and is pronounced accordingly. (See § 93.)

97. **y** has the force of a consonant at the beginning of words of foreign origin. It is then called *yuh* in spelling for pronunciation.

---

* i is distinctly sounded in **cuistre, Juillet, ouillière.**

PRACTICE.

TWENTY-FIRST EXERCISE. *Vingt-et-unième exercice.*

<table>
<tr><td>⁷ ³ ⁶ ⁷ ⁶
Il le pay-ait,*
eel luh peh yeh.</td><td>he paid him.</td><td>⁶ ⁴ ² ⁶ ⁷ ⁶ [thick.
Ell-le gras-sey-ait, she spoke
ehl' grah seh yeh.</td></tr>
<tr><td>¹² ⁵ ⁶ ⁷ ¹⁵
nous l'es-say-ons,
noo la seh yōn.</td><td>we try it.</td><td>¹⁰ ⁵ ¹⁷ ⁷ ¹
tu net-toy-as, thou didst clean.
tü na tweh yä.</td></tr>
<tr><td>¹² ⁵ ¹⁰ ⁷ ⁷ ⁵
vous l'es-suy-ez,
voo la sü ee ya.</td><td>[off.
you wipe it</td><td>¹ ⁶ ¹⁷ ⁷ ⁵
a-ter-moy-er, to delay.
ä tehr mweh ya.</td></tr>
<tr><td>¹² ¹³ ⁷ ⁷ ⁵
vous l'en-vi-iez,
voo lān vee ya.</td><td>you envy him.</td><td>¹⁶ ⁷ ¹ ¹ ¹³
un ya-ta-gan, a yataghan.
ūn yä tä gān.</td></tr>
</table>

Il le payait, nous l'essayons, vous l'essuyez, vous l'enviiez, elle grasseyait, tu nettoyas, atermoyer, un yatagan.

---

* y preceded by a vowel forms a syllable with that vowel; but, having the value of two i's, the first, *only*, combines with the preceding vowel-letter to represent either a pure vowel or a diphthongal sound. The second i, which takes the liquid sound *yuh*, goes over to the next syllable; and, if that syllable begins with a vowel, a diphthongal sound (*i.e.*, two distinct vowel-sounds uttered in one emission of the voice) is formed. In accordance with this rule, **payait, atermoyer, essayons, grasseyait,** &c., will be spelled: puh eh **pah,** ȳuh eh **yeh, pehyeh;** ă, tuh eh ruh **tehr, ătehr,** muh weh **mweh, ătehrmweh,** ȳuh a ȳa, **ătehrmwehȳa;** a, suh eh **seh, aseh,** ȳuh ōn **ȳōn, asehȳōn;** gruh ah **grah,** suh eh **seh, grahseh,** ȳuh eh **ȳeh, grahsehȳeh,** &c.

Obs.— In the syllabification of words containing the y preceded by a vowel, the division must, of course, be made after the **y**; but it should be remembered that, since only one i sound belongs to the first syllable, there is one to spare (the *yuh* sound); and the latter should be named and fully pronounced in spelling the second syllable.

ă, as; ah, āh, father; uh, ermine; ŏ or ', move; a, late; eh, met; ēh, there; ee, police; ŏ, nor; o, also; ō, no; ŭ, constitution; eū, first; oo, too; ān, want; ĭn, Yankee; ōn, don't; ūn, grunt; weh, wear; wah, water; ḡ, go; zh, glazier; ḡn, singing; ȳ, yes.

THEORY.

TWENTY-SECOND LESSON. *Vingt-deuxième leçon.*

VOWEL LETTERS AND SOUNDS (*continued*).

98. CONCERNING THE LETTER y. — In the case of three successive i sounds (which occur in the ending of some verbs), the first two are pronounced according to the rules already given. The third is named and sounded ee, and, together with the second, which begins the syllable and is named *yuh*, precisely represents the sound yie of *yield*.

99. In nearly all proper names, the y has the value of a consonant, and is pronounced as in *yes*.

Also in a few other words; such as, bayadère, bayonnette, berruyer, bruya, mayonnaise, bruyant, bruyamment,[*] &c. M. de la Boulaye is pronounced *laboulai ;* and La Haye, *la hai.*

OBS. — When y has the value of a consonant, it naturally begins the syllable.

100. EIGHTH VOWEL-SOUND. — When o does not represent the last sound heard in a word, it is sounded as in *nor*.

101. o, eo, and au, before r, have also the same sound. u, in the termination *um* of words borrowed from the Latin, has the sound of o in *none*.

102. In a few words, such as, augmenter, auxiliaire, cautère, mauvais, mauviette, auberge, Paul, Saul, paupière, naufrage, ausculter, austral, austère, cautèle, and a few others, au, although not followed by r, is, however, pronounced as o in *nor*.

103. NINTH VOWEL-SOUND. — o, without accent, is sounded as in *also* (semi-long). 1°. When it represents the last sound heard in a word. 2°. In the compounds and derivatives of words ending in os, provided s be silent in the primitive. 3°. Before s single followed by a vowel. 4°. Before tion. 5°. In the termination one of words derived from the Greek.

---

[*] Bayer, boyard, brayer, brayette, brayon, cipaye, fayard, fayence, gayac, payen, begayement, zézaye, cacaoyer, caloyer, goyave.

PRACTICE.

TWENTY-SECOND EXERCISE. *Vingt-deuxième exercice.*

12 10 17 11 15	[harshly.		1 10 7 6 4		
Nous ru-doy-ions,	we treated		**La Bru-yè-re,**	La Bruyère.	
noo rü dweh ÿee ōn.			lă brü ÿehr'.		
12 5 10 7 7 7 5			1 7 11		
vous es-suy-iez,	you wiped off.		**Ba-yeux,**	Bayeux.	
voo za sü ee ÿee a.			bă ÿēū.		
5 6 7 1 4	[women.		1 7 4		
les pay-san-nes,*	the country		**Ca-yes,**	Cayes.	
la peh ee zăn'.			kă ÿĕ.		
4 6 7			8 4 8 6 4		
le pays,*	the country.		**no-tre au-ber-ge,**	our inn.	
l' peh ee..			nŏtr' ŏ behrzh'.		
1 5 1 8			4 9 9 7 5		
al-lez ail-leurs,†	go elsewhere.		**le dos, dos-sier,**	the back, brief.	
ă la ză ÿeehr.			l' do, do see a.		
5 1 6 7 4			1 5 8 7 15		
les ab-bay-es,‡	the abbeys.		**la dé-vo-tion,**	the devotion.	
la ză beh ee.			lă da vo see ōn.		
8 6 4			1 1 9 4		
mor-tel-le, §	mortal.		**l'a-ma-zo-ne,**	the female rider.	
mŏr tehl'.			lă mă zon'.		

Nous rudoyions, vous essuyiez, les paysannes, le pays, allez ailleurs, les abbayes, mortelle, La Bruyère, Bayeux, Cayes, notre auberge, le dos, dossier, la dévotion, l'amazone.

---

* **Les paysannes, le pays,** will be spelled: luh a la, puh eh peh, ee pehee, zuh ă ză, peheeză, nuh uh nuh, peheezăn', la pehee-zăn'; luh uh luh, puh eh peh, ee pehee, l'pehee.

† When several words are connected in sense, they may be divided and spelled as one long word. Example: **allons ailleurs**: ă, luh ōn lōn, ălōn, zuh ă ză, ălōnză, yuh uh ruh yuhr, ălōnzăyuhr, &c.

‡ **Les abbayes** will be spelled: luh a la, zuh ă za, lază, buh eh beh, lazăbeh, ee, lazăbehee.

§ When a suffix commencing with a vowel is added to a word ending with a consonant, the consonant resumes its full value, and becomes the initial of the next syllable, — **mort, mor-tel-le,** &c.

ă, as; ah, ăh, father; uh, ermine; ĕ or ', move; a, late; eh, met; ēh, there; ee, police; ŏ, nor; o, also; ō, no; ŭ, constitution; ēū, first; oo, too; ān, want; m̄, Yankee; ōn, don't; ūn, grunt; weh, wear; wah, water; ḡ, go; zh, glazier; ḡn, singing; ÿ, yes.

THEORY.

TWENTY-THIRD LESSON. *Vingt-troisième leçon.*

VOWEL LETTERS AND SOUNDS (*continued*).

104. By reason of etymology, **o** is sounded as in *no* in **atome, épitome, hippodrome, mome, axiome, idiome, tome,** and a few other words ending in **tome,** and seldom used.

105. The combinations **eo, au, eau,** are pronounced as **o** in *also*, except before **r**. (See § 101.)

106. Double **o** is generally pronounced as single.

107. **ô** and **eô** are sounded as **o** in *no*. The lips should protrude a little in uttering the long **o**.

108. TENTH VOWEL-SOUND. — **û** is long when the accent is an etymological trace, a mark of contraction; as in **chûte, flûte, sûr, mûr, &c.,** which formerly were written, *cheute, fluste, seur, meur,* &c.: but when the circumflex accent is used to distinguish words of the same spelling, but of a different meaning, there is no difference between **u** and **û**, either in the quality or quantity of the sound: **dû,** *owed;* **du,** *of the:* **tû,** *been silent;* **tu,** *thou;* **crû,** *grown;* **cru,** *believed;* &c.

109. **ue** final, and **eue, eu,** throughout the verb **avoir,** *to have,* are also pronounced as **u** in *constitution*.

110. When **u** is used as an orthographic letter after **g** and **c**, it is silent. Its function is to indicate that **g** and **c** retain their hard sound.

111. In the verbs of the first conjugation ending in **guer,** the **u**, which is retained throughout the conjugation, is silent. But in the verb **arguer** the **u** forms a distinct syllable, and is fully sounded, in all the tenses and persons of that verb.

112. **u,** preceded by combined consonants (**bl, fr, pl,** &c.), and followed by any other vowel than the mute **e**, forms a distinct syllable with the consonants: **le con-flu-ent, il con-clu-ait, le gru-au, la tru-an-de-rie.**

PRACTICE.

TWENTY-THIRD EXERCISE. *Vingt-troisième exercice.*

Sau-ve gar-de, sov' gārd'.	safeguard.	Je le cueil-le, zh' luh kuhy'.	I gather it.
la roy-au-té, lă rweh yo ta.	the royalty.	la tru-an-de-rie, lă trü ānd' ree.	the vagrancy.
Guil-lau-me, ḡee yom'.	William.	l'in-flu-en-ce, lĭn flŭ āns'.	the influence.
l'au-to-ri-té, lo tŏ ree ta.	the authority.	il con-ju-gua, eel kōn zhŭ gă.	he conjugated.
Wa-ter-loo, vă tehr lo.	Waterloo.	nous ar-gu-ons, noo zăr gü ōn.	we argue.
rou-geaud, roo zho.	red-faced.	u-ne blu-et-te, ŭn' blŭ eht'.	a spark.
la geô-le, lă zhōl'.	the jail.	les im-pôts, la zĭn pŏ.	the taxes.
vo-tre flû-te, vŏtr' flŭt'.	your flute.	la Drô-me, lă drōm'.	the Drome.
vous l'eû-tes, voo lŭt'.	you had it.	l'hip-po-dro-me, lee pŏ drom'.	the hippo-[drome.

Sauve garde, la royauté, Guillaume, l'autorité, Waterloo, rougeaud, la geôle, votre flûte, vous l'eûtes, je le cueille, la truanderie, l'influence, il conjugua, nous arguons, une bluette, les impôts, la Drôme, l'hippodrome.

ă, as; ah, āh, father; uh, ermine; ŏ or ', move; a, late; eh, met; ēh, there; ee, police; ŏ, nor; o, also; ō, no; ŭ, constitution; ēū, first; oo, too; ān, want; ĭn, Yankee; ōn, don't; ūn, grunt; weh, wear; wah, water; ḡ, go; zh, glazier; ḡn, singing; ȳ, yes.

THEORY.

TWENTY-FOURTH LESSON. *Vingt-quatrième leçon.*

VOWEL LETTERS AND SOUNDS (*continued*).

113. CONCERNING THE LETTER u. — The u is sounded oo (as in *too*) in **Fiume, Calatayud, Yucatan, Ucayal, Udine, Estramadure, Uhr** (in Chaldea), and in the syllables **gua** and **qua** of a few words given further on.

114. u is distinctly sounded in **cuistre, juillet,** and **cuiller,** which is familiarly called *cu-yer*.

115. **Puff** and **turf**, without analogy in French, are pronounced *peuf* and *teurf*; and **curaçoa** is pronounced *cuiraço*.

116. The u of other words borrowed from foreign languages has assumed the French pronunciation with naturalization: thus **club** is not pronounced *cleub, clab,* or *clob,* but clŭb.

117. ELEVENTH VOWEL-SOUND. — The combinations **eue, œu,** represent the eleventh sound, but only when they *are not* followed by b, f, l, il, n not final, p, r, and v.

118. **eu,** in the body of a word, is submitted to the same rule; but, at the beginning of a word, it is sounded as i in *first* (11th sound) before ALL letters.

*119. eû represents the eleventh sound in all cases.

120. The termination **fs** is silent in **œufs** and **bœufs,** and the combination **œu** assumes the 11th sound; but, in the singular **œuf** and **bœuf,** the f is fully sounded, and **œu** is regularly pronounced as **e** in **e**rmine.

121. In **meunier, eu** is pronounced as i in *first*.

122. TWELFTH VOWEL-SOUND. — **ou, oue** final, **où,** and **août,** represent the 12th vowel-sound, which is identical with that of **oo** in *too*.

123. **oui** before l liquid is also pronounced as **oo** in *too*.

PRACTICE.

TWENTY-FOURTH EXERCISE. *Vingt-quatrième exercice.*

Ū-ne é-meu-te,* a riot.		La bouil-loi-re,†	the kettle.
ŭ na meūt'.		lă boo y̨wehr'.	
il pleut,	it rains.	la ci-trouil-le,†	the pumpkin.
eel pleū.		lă see trooy̨'.	
Eu-gé-nie,	Eugenia.	vo-tre ou-vra-ge,	your work.
eū zha nee.		vŏ tr'oo vrăzh'.	
l'eu-pho-nie,	the euphony.	a-ge-nouil-lez-vous, kneel down.	
leū fŏ nee.		ăzh' noo y̨a voo.	
la yeu-se,	the holm oak.	la voû-te,	the vault.
lă y̨eūz'.		lă voot'.	

Une émeute, il pleut, Eugénie, l'euphonie, la yeuse, la bouilloire, la citrouille, votre ouvrage, agenouillez-vous, la voûte.

---

* The e final unaccented and preceded by a vowel is silent. Preceded by a consonant, as in **émeute, voiture, globe,** &c., it is semimute, as in English in *move, lake,* &c. But when, in the latter case, the next word begins with a vowel or a mute h, and no pause, however short, should be made between the two words because of their intimate connection in sense, then the final e of the first word becomes silent, and the two words are so blended as to become one long word, which should be divided and pronounced accordingly. Example: **une émeute, la voiture ârriva**; divided and pronounced, u-né-meu-te, la voi-tu-rar-ri-va.

† **La bouilloire, la citrouille,** &c., will be spelled: luh ă lă, buh oo boo, y̨uh weh y̨weh, booy̨weh, ruh uh ruh, booy̨wehr', lă booy̨wehr'; luh ă lă, suh ee see, truh oo troo, seetroo, y̨uh uh y̨uh, seetrooy̨, lă seetrooy̨; &c.

ă, as; ah, äh, father; uh, ermine; ŏ or ', move; a, late; eh, met; ēh, there; ee, police; ŏ, nor; o, also; ō, no; ŭ, constitution; eū, first; oo, too; an̄, want; īn, Yankee; on̄, don't; un̄, grunt; weh, wear; wah, water; g, go; zh, glazier; gn̄, singing; y̨, yes.

THEORY.

TWENTY-FIFTH LESSON. *Vingt-cinquième leçon.*

VOWEL LETTERS AND SOUNDS (*continued*).

124. NASAL SOUNDS. — Various combinations, or coalitions, of letters, besides **an, in, on, un**, are used to represent each one of our nasal sounds.

125. As a general rule, **m** and **n** preceded by a vowel in the same syllable form a nasal sound with that vowel: hence, nasal sounds occur at the beginning, in the middle, and at the end of words.

126. In words borrowed from foreign languages which do not admit nasal sounds, **m** and **n** after a vowel retain their full value as consonants, and are pronounced accordingly.

127. **m** has the same value as **n** in effecting the nasalization of the preceding vowel.

128. The FIRST NASAL SOUND, which is the thirteenth sound in our scale (**an** in *want*), is represented by **an, am, aen, aon, en, em, ean,** and **œn**.

129. **aen** is pronounced **an** in *Caen;* but in *Caennais, Caennaise,* the **n** being doubled, the first is silent, consequently no nasalization occurs, and these two words are pronounced *ca-nais, ca-nai-se.*

130. In the following words, **aon** is sounded **an**: **faon, paon, Saint-Haon, Craon, Laon**; but the derivatives, **paonne, paonneau, Laonnais, faonner,** are pronounced *pa-ne, pa-neau, La-nais, fa-ner.*

131. **ean** is also sounded **an**; and the nasal sound likewise disappears when the **n** is doubled. **Jeanne, Jeannette,** are pronounced *Ja-ne, Ja-net-te.*

132. The word **en** (pronoun and preposition) has always the nasal sound (**an** in *want*), which it retains before all letters, even when, in its prepositional character, it is united to and becomes an integral part of a word.

PRACTICE.

TWENTY-FIFTH EXERCISE. *Vingt-cinquième exercice.*

Saint Jean, sān zhān.	Saint John.	Jean-net-te, zhă neht'.	Jennet.
le Gro-en-land, l' grŏ ān lān.	Greenland.	en-har-dir, ān ăr deer.	to embolden.
Rouen, roo ān.	Rouen.	en-no-blir, ān nŏ bleer.	to ennoble.
l'em-ploi, lān plweh.	the employment.	en-i-vrer, ān nee vra.	to intoxicate.
l'em-bar-ras, lān bă rah.	the encumbrance.	en-clou-er, ān kloo a.	to spike (guns).
Am-broi-se, ān brwehz'.	Ambrose.	en-or-gueil-lir, ān nŏr ğuh yeer.	to render proud.
il prend, eel prān.	he takes.	l'en-nui, lān nüee.	the weariness.
le faon, Laon, l' fān, lān.	the fawn, Laon.	en-har-na-cher, ān ăr nă sha.	to harness.

Saint-Jean, le Groenland, Rouen, l'emploi, l'embarras, Ambroise, il prend, le faon, Laon, Jeannette, enhardir, ennoblir, enivrer, enclouer, enorgueillir, l'ennui, enharnacher.

ă, as; ah, âh, father; uh, ermine; ĕ or ', move; a, late; eh, met; ēh, there; ee, police; ŏ, nor; o, also; ō, no; ŭ, constitution; eū, first; oo, too; ān, want; īn, Yankee; ōn, don't; ūn, grunt; weh, **wear**; wah, **water**; ḡ, go; zh, glazier; ḡn, singing; ȳ, yes.

THEORY.

TWENTY-SIXTH LESSON. *Vingt-sixième leçon.*

VOWEL LETTERS AND SOUNDS (*continued*).

133. THIRTEENTH VOWEL-SOUND. — **en**, preceded by **i, y,** or **é**, is sounded **in** (as **an** in *Yankee*); but it retains its proper sound **an** (as **an** in *want*) in the following words and in their derivatives: l'audience, coefficient, efficient, clientèle, émollient, expérience, impatient, patience, récipient, science, client, conscience, escient, expédient, inconvénient, orient, prescience, quotient, récipiendaire, patient.

134. **em** is pronounced in in a few words of foreign origin, — sempiternel, Wurtemberg, &c.

135. In some proper names and words, mostly from the Greek, **em** is sounded **èm** (*ehm*), — Memphis, Lemnos, &c.

136. FOURTEENTH VOWEL-SOUND. — The second nasal sound, whose equivalent we find in **an** of *Yankee*, is represented by **in, im, ain, aim, ein, eim, yn, ym,** and **en** final or after **i** or **é**. (See § 134.)

137. FIFTEENTH VOWEL-SOUND. — The third nasal sound (as **on** in *don't*) is represented by **on, aon, eon, om, um,** and **un**.

138. The **e** of **eon** is an orthographic letter, used after **g**, to indicate that the **g** retains its soft sound, as **z** in *glazier*, before **o** (also before **a** and **u**): the **e** is therefore silent.

139. The first syllable of **conné, connotatif,** is, by reason of etymology, slightly nasalized.

140. The combinations **um** and **un** are pronounced **on** in the following words: résumption, rumb, punch, Dunkerque, Humbold, unguifère, unguis.

141. SIXTEENTH VOWEL-SOUND. — Only three combinations represent the fourth and last nasal sound, — **un, um,** and **eun**.

PRACTICE.

TWENTY–SIXTH EXERCISE. *Vingt-sixième exercice.*

De-main, d' miñ.	to-morrow.	Em-ma-nuel, ehm mă nü ehl'.	Emmanuel.
les A-mé-ri-cains,* la ză ma ree kiñ.	the Ameri-[cans.	dé-cem-vir, da sehm veer.	decemvir.
un es-saim, uñ na siñ.	a swarm of bees.	Nem-rod, nehm röd.	Nimrod.
nous e-xi-geons, noo za gzee zhoñ.	we require.	Jé-ru-sa-lem, zha rü ză lehm.	Jerusalem.
un plon-geon, uñ ploñ zhoñ.	a diver.	Bé-thlé-em, ba tla ehm.	Bethlehem.
ins-cri-re, ins kreer'.	to inscribe.	Pha-ra-on, fă ră oñ.	Pharaoh.
les par-fums, la pär füñ.	the perfumes.	le vain-queur, l' viñ kuhr.	the victor.
à jeun, ă zhüñ.	fasting.	cin-quiè-me, siñ kee ehm'.	fifth.

Demain, les Américains, un essaim, nous exigeons, un plongeon, inscrire, les parfums, à jeun, Emmanuel, décemvir, Nemrod, Jérusalem, Béthléem, Pharaon, le vainqueur, cinquième.

---

* Les Américains will be spelled: luh a la, zuh ă ză, muh a ma, zăma, ruh ee ree, zămaree, kuh iñ kiñ, zămareekiñ, lă zămareekiñ.

ă, as; ah, âh, father; uh, ermine; ĕ or ', move; a, late; eh, met; êh, there; ee, police; ŏ, nor; o, also; ō, no; ŭ, constitution; eū, first; oo, too; añ, want; iñ, Yankee; oñ, don't; uñ, grunt; weh, wear; wah, water; ḡ, go; zh, glazier; ḡn, singing; ȳ, yes.

THEORY.

TWENTY-SEVENTH LESSON. *Vingt-septième leçon.*

VOWEL LETTERS AND SOUNDS (*continued*).

142. NASAL SOUNDS. — The consonants which follow a nasal sound in the same syllable are generally silent, but **s** is always sounded.

143. Final consonants preceded by a nasal sound are silent; except in **sphinx, sens, lynx, cinq, Hasting**.

144. **Monsieur**, in which the nasal sound is suppressed, has this peculiar pronunciation, — *muh-see-eū*.

145. **on** forms a distinct syllable in **Phaon, Pharaon, Demaphoon**.

146. All words ending in **um** have been borrowed from the Latin; and **u** of **um** final is pronounced as **o** in *nor*, — **m** retains its natural sound. But **parfum** (which is not borrowed, but *derived* from the Latin *per fumus*), the only exception, has the nasal sound as **un** in *grunt*.

OBS. — When a word ending with **n** is intimately connected in sense with that which follows, and the latter begins with a vowel, the two words, according to rule, are run together into one word. The **n**, becoming *de facto* the initial consonant of a syllable, ought regularly to lose its character as a nasal letter, and resume its natural sound; but such is not always the case, — the nasalization of the **n** does not disappear entirely, except in very rapid conversation. The **n** has therefore two functions. 1°. It retains the quality of a nasal letter, and acts accordingly in the syllable to which it belongs. 2°. Its natural sound is restored, and is carried to the next word: thus, **son offre, bien unis, mon oncle**, are pronounced *son noffre, bien nunis, mon noncle*, &c.

147. SEVENTEENTH VOWEL-SOUND. — The combinations **oi, oî, oy, oie, eoi**, represent the 17th sound, which is equivalent to that of **wea** in *wear*.

PRACTICE.

TWENTY-SEVENTH EXERCISE. *Vingt-septième exercice.*

³Le ¹⁴sphinx, luh sfĭnks.	the sphinx.	¹⁰U-⁴ne ¹⁷boî-⁴te, ŭn' bwĕht'.	a box.
⁵lĕs ¹par-¹⁶fums, la păr fŭn.	the perfumes.	⁹nos ¹⁷foy-⁷⁵ers, no fweh ya.	our firesides.
¹⁵son ¹al-⁸bum, sōn năl bŏm.	her album.	⁴le ⁵net-¹⁷toy-⁷a-¹⁴ge, l' na tweh yăzh'.	the cleaning.
¹⁵mon ¹³en-¹³fant, mōn năn făn.	my child.	⁴le ⁷vil-¹la-¹⁷geois, l' wee lă zhweh.	the villager.
¹⁵son ¹a-⁷mie, sōn nă mee.	his friend.	¹⁶un ¹⁷noy-⁷⁹au, ŭn nweh yo.	a cling-stone.
⁸mo-¹⁰nu-¹³men-¹tal, mŏ nŭ măn tăl.	monumental.	⁵dé-¹⁷ploy-⁷⁵er, da plweh ya.	to unfold.
¹³Ven-³dre-⁷di, văn druh dee.	Friday.	⁵les ¹⁷oies, la zweh.	the geese.
¹³en-¹³sem-⁴ble, ăn sănbl'.	together.	¹⁷Troie, trweh.	Troy.

Le sphinx, les parfums, son album, mon enfant, son amie, monumental, vendredi, ensemble, une boîte, nos foyers, le nettoyage, le villageois, un noyau, déployer, les oies, Troie.

ă, as; ah, äh, father; uh, ermine; ĕ or ', move; a, late; eh, met; ēh, there; ee, police; ŏ, nor; o, also; ō, no; ŭ, constitution; eū, first; oo, too; ān, want; m̄, Yankee; ōn, don't; ŭn, grunt; weh, wear; wah, water; g, go; zh, glazier; ḡn, singing; ȳ, yes.

THEORY.

TWENTY-EIGHTH LESSON. *Vingt-huitième leçon.*

DIPHTHONGS.

148. DEFINITION. — A French diphthong is the close union of TWO VOWEL-SOUNDS (and not *two vowel-letters*, as in English) in one syllable.

OBS. — The word *diphthong* (δίφθογγος) etymologically signifies *twice sounded*, or double sound or voice. It is really a syllable composed of *two distinct vowel-sounds*, pronounced in one emission of the voice, and modified by the simultaneous movements of the organs of speech.

149. The two vowel-sounds which form the diphthong must be heard distinctly, though pronounced in one explosion of the voice.

150. A diæresis is the division of a group of vowels into two syllables.*

OBS. — The ear alone is judge of the diphthong. Two, three, or four vowel-letters may be written in succession; but, if one sound only is heard, it is a *vowel-sound*, not a diphthong. Hence in **laie, chaud, beau**, we have mere vowel-sounds, each one of which might be represented by one vowel-letter alone, — thus, *lè, shô, bô;* but in **fiacre, pied, biais, oui, ouais**, we have diphthongal sounds, because each syllable includes two distinct vowel-sounds, — thus, *fi-a-cre, pi-ed, bi-è, ou-i, ou-è*.

151. The first sound of a diphthong is always pronounced rapidly: the voice dwells upon the second sound only, because the position of the organs which form this second sound has succeeded suddenly to that which had formed the first.

OBS. — Since diphthongs consist of two vowel-sounds, they are necessarily long by nature.

---

* The English i of *mine* represents a true diæresis; **ian** in *brilliantness* forms a diphthong; while **eau** of *beau* is a mere vowel-sound.

THEORY AND PRACTICE.

TWENTY-EIGHTH EXERCISE. *Vingt-huitième exercice.*

DIPHTHONGS, WITH THEIR PRONUNCIATION.

7 1   7 1   7 2   7 5   7 5   7 5   7 5   7 5   7 5   7 5   7 5   7 6   7 6   7 6   7 6
ia, ya; ia; ie, ye, yai, ied, ier, iez, yer, yez; ie, ye, iè, yè
ee ă, yă, ee ah, ee a, ya, ya, ee a, ee a, ee a, ya, ya, ee eh, yeh, ee eh, yeh,

7 6   7 6   7 13   7 13   7 13   7 14   7 14   7 11   7 11   7 3   7 8   7 8   7 9   7 9
iai, yai; ian, yan, ien; ien, yen; ieu, yeu; yeur; io, yo; io, yau;
ee eh, yeh, ee an, yan, ee an, ee in, y in, ee eu, yeu, yuhr, ee ŏ, yŏ, ee o, yo,

7 15   7 15   7 12   7 12   7 10   12 2   12 6   12 6   12 6   12 14   12 2   12 6   12 6
ion, yon; iou, you; yu; oa, oe, oé, oê; oin; oua, oue, ouai;
ee on, yon, ee oo, yoo, yŭ, oo ah, oo eh, oo eh, oo ăh, oo in, oo ah, oo eh, oo eh,

12 7   12 13   12 13   12 14   12 2   10 6   10 5   10 7   10 7   10 14
oui; ouan, ouen; ouin; ua; ue; ué; ui, uy; uin; and, with the
oo ee, oo an, oo an, oo in, oo ah, ü eh, ü a, ü ee, ü ee, ü in,

17   17   17
irregular oi, oie, oy, — 55.
weh, weh, weh,

GENERAL OBSERVATIONS. — The two diphthongs **oin** and **ouin** are pronounced nearly alike. The only difference is that the o sound is a little more distinct in *oin*, while in *ouin* the sound oo (as in *too*) predominates. **ouin** is pronounced somewhat like **uain** in *quaint;* the French sound having more volume than the English.

The rules which are given in the following pages for the distinction of the diphthongs from diæreses are by no means invariable. In some respects, poetry differs from prose in its pronunciation, and, in the license which is generally granted to poets, the rules may sometimes be reversed: they at times make a diæresis where common usage recognizes but a diphthong, and *vice versa*. But what is allowable in poetry, provided the verse be otherwise good, should not be indulged in elsewhere; and, besides, rules well established and generally followed should not be violated.

In conclusion, I will say that the diæreses are more frequent and more marked in poetry than in prose; more accused in declamation than in reading, and in reading more than in conversation: to dwell too much on the separation of the syllables which enter into the composition of a word would, at times, be pedantry.

THEORY.

TWENTY-NINTH LESSON. *Vingt-neuvième leçon.*

DIPHTHONGS (*continued*).

OBS. — Each one of the two sounds composing a diphthong is individually subjected, as regards its pronunciation, to all the rules which have been previously given for the pronunciation of the vowel-sounds.

152. The diphthongs are formed by the combination, —

1°. Of a simple vowel with another simple vowel.
2°. Of a simple vowel with a vowel-sound represented by several letters, preceding or following that vowel.
3°. Of two vowel-sounds, each one represented by several letters.
4°. Of simple or compound vowels with a nasal sound, pronounced in one syllable.

153. All diphthongs begin with one of the letters **i, y, o, u.**

OBS. — The same diphthongal sound may be represented by diverse combinations of letters.

154. **oi, oie, oy,** may also be considered as irregular diphthongs.

155. TWO DIPHTHONGS IN SUCCESSION. — When **y** is preceded by a vowel, it has the value of two i's. If it be at the same time followed by another vowel or by a combination of vowels (which is almost always the case), a diphthongal syllable will result, which is composed of the second i sound of **y** and the following vowel-sound. But the first i sound of **y** may also form a diphthong with the preceding vowel; hence it follows that two diphthongal sounds may come in succession. Such is the case when **y** is preceded by **u** or **o**; thus, **tuyau, essuyer, royal,** &c., which might be written, *tui-iau, essui-ier, roi-ial,* &c.

THEORY AND PRACTICE.

TWENTY-NINTH EXERCISE. *Vingt-neuvième exercice.*

156. **ia** is a diphthong in the following words only:—

Di̥a̤! di̥a̤-cre̤, gee-ho! deacon.	Plé-ia-de̤,	Pleiades.
dee ă deeă kr'.	pla ee ăd'.	
[thing.		
fia-cre̤, liard, hack, half-a-far-	dia-ble̤,	devil.
fee ăkr', lee ăr.	dee ahbl'.	
[dollar.		
piaf-fe̤, pias-tre̤, ostentatious,	dia-blo-tin,	devilkin.
pee ăf', pee ăstr'.	deeah blŏ tiñ.	

and in their compounds and derivatives.

157. **ya** is a diphthong everywhere:—

Nous pay-â-mes, we paid.	Il noy-a,	he drowned.
noo peh yăm'.	eel nweh yă.	

158. **ié** is not a diphthong, but a diæresis.

1°. After two consonants, the last of which is **l** or **r**.
2°. In the participles of verbs whose infinitive terminates in **ier**.
3°. In the derivatives of **quiet** and **inquiet**.
4°. In the words ending in **été**.

It is a diphthong everywhere else:—

Les a-mi-tiés, the friendships.	La pa-rié-tai-re,	the wall-wort.
la ză mee teea.	lă pă reea tehr'.	
les hié-ro-gly-phes, the hiero-[glyphs.	la dié-ré-se,	the diæresis.
la zeearŏ gleef'.	lă dee rehz'.	

159. **yé** is a diphthong everywhere.

Oc-troy-é, granted.	Es-suy-é,	wiped off.
ŏk trweh ya.	a sŭee ya.	

ă, as; ah, âh, father; uh, ermine; ĕ or ', move; a, late; eh, met; ēh, there; ee, police; ŏ, nor; o, also; ō, no; ŭ, constitution; ēū, first; oo, too; a͞n, want; i͞n, Yankee; o͞n, don't; u͞n, grunt; weh, **w**ear; wah, **w**ater; ḡ, go; zh, glazier; ḡn, singing; ȳ, **y**es.

THEORY AND PRACTICE.

160. ied is a diphthong in the following words, in their compounds and derivatives:—

Pied, il s'as-sied, foot, he sits [down. | Il sied, it becomes.
pee a, eel sa see a. | eel see a.

161. Obs.—There is no diphthong in a group of letters beginning with **i**, when the **i** is preceded by two consonants the second of which is **l** or **r**: such a group forms two syllables.

162. ier, iez, are diphthongs, except in the verbs ending in the infinitive in **ier**, in the adverb **hier**, and in **riez, riiez** (of *rire*), also when **iez** is preceded by **y**:—

Le doig-tier, the finger-stall. | Vous -fi-nis-siez, you finished.
l' dweh tee a. | voo fee nee see a.

l'es-ca-lier, the stair-case. | vous é-tiez, you were.
las kă lee a. | voo za tee a.

163. yai, yer, yez, are diphthongs everywhere:—

J'ap-puy-ai, I pressed down. | Vous broy-ez, you crush.
zhă püee ya. | voo brweh ya.

se dé-sen-nuy-er, to divert [one's self. | qui que vous so-yez, whomso- [ever you may be.
s' da zăn nüee ya. | kee k' voo sweh ya.

164. ie is a diphthong in—

Aïe! huïe! oh! oh! | Ciel, fiel, miel, sky, gall, honey.
ăyĕ ăyĕ. | see ehl, fee ehl, mee ehl.

bief, fief, re-lief, mill-dam, fief, [relievo. | plu-riel, plural.
bee ehf, fee ehf, ruh lee ehf. | plü ree ehl.

In the combination **iet**, except in **quiet, inquiet**.

As-siet-te, miet-te, plate, crumb. | Ser-viet-te, napkin.
ă see eht', mee eht'. | sehr vee eht'.

ă, as; ah, āh, father; uh, ermine; ĕ or ', move; a, late; eh, met; ēh, there; ee, police; ŏ, nor; o, also; ō, no; ŭ, constitution; ēu, first; oo, too; añ, want; īn, Yankee; ōn, don't; ūn, grunt; weh, wear; wah, water; g̃, go; zh, glazier; g̃ñ, singing; ȳ, yes.

THEORY AND PRACTICE.

165. **ie** before **nn** is always diphthongal in the tenses of the verbs ending in **enir**. This group of letters (**ienn**), on the contrary, forms generally a diæresis in the feminine of adjectives ending in **ien** in the masculine:—

Qu'il vien-ne, let him come. | Ma-gi-ci-en-ne, magician (f.).
keel vee ehn'. | mă zhee cee ehn'.
qu'el-le ob-tien-ne, let her ob- [tain. | Vé-ni-ti-en-ne, Venitian (f.).
kehl' ŏb tee ehn'. | va nee see ehn'.

166. **ye** is a diphthong, except when **e** final *is silent*:—

La-fa-yet-te, Lafayette. | Ab-bay-e, la Hay-e, Abbey, la [Haye.
lă fă yeht'. | ă beh ee, lă eh.

167. **iè** and **yè** are diphthongs everywhere:—

Lu-miè-re, light. | Pre-miè-re, first (f.).
lŭ mee' ehr'. | pruh mee ehr'.
la bru-yè-re, the heath. | gru-yè-re, gruyere cheese.
lă brŭ yehr'. | grŭ yehr.

168. **iai** is a diphthong in **biais, biaiser,** and **bréviaire**, only. **yai** is a diphthong everywhere:—

Biais, biai-ser, slant, to lean. | Bré-viai-re, breviary.
bee eh, bee eh za. | bra vee ehr'.
il gras-sey-ait, he spoke thick. | je-ba-lay-ais, I swept.
eel grah seh yeh. | zh' bă leh yeh.

169. **ian** is a diphthong in **diantre** and **viande** only. **yan** is a diphthong everywhere:—

170. **ien**, pronounced **ian** (*ee an*), forms always a diæresis: **ien** is a diphthong:—

La fa-ïen-ce, the china-ware. | Pa-ti-ent, patient.
lă fă ee āns'. | pă see āṅ.

ă, as; ah, âh, father; uh, ermine; ĕ or ', move; a, late; eh, met; ēh, there; ee, police; ŏ, nor; o, also; ō, no; ŭ, constitution; ēū, first; oo, too; āṅ, want; īṅ, Yankee; ōṅ, don't; ūṅ, grunt; weh, wear; wah, water; ḡ, go; zh, glazier; ḡn, singing; ȳ, yes.

THEORY AND PRACTICE.

171. **ien** (pronounced *ee in*), at the end of words, is a diphthong:—

1°. In the verbs ending in **enir**,—**viens, maintiens, souvient**, &c.
2°. In nouns as **bien, chien, maintien**, &c. Except in **lien** and generally in proper names of men,—**Bastien**, &c.
3°. In the adverbs **bien, combien**.

ien is also a diphthong (in the middle of words) in the future and conditional of the verbs ending in **enir**,— **il conviendra, tu retiendrait**.

On the contrary, **ien** forms always a diæresis, in adjectives, especially in those which designate the country or the profession: ex., **Lydien, Sicilien, mécanicien**, &c.

However, **ien** is diphthong in **ancien, chrétien, faubourien, plébéien, le mien, le tien, le sien**, and **autrichien**.

172. **yen** is a diphthong everywhere:—

¹⁶ ⁷ ¹⁷ ^{7 14}
Un ci-toy-en,   a citizen.
ŭn see tweh yĭn.

⁵ ¹⁷ ^{7 14}
Les moy-ens,   the means.
la mweh yĭn.

173. **ieu** is always a diphthong in nouns, but represents a diæresis in adjectives and attributes, except in **vieux** and in the adverb **mieux**.

174. **ïeu, yeu**, and **yeur** are diphthongs everywhere:—

^{7 11} ⁵ ^{7 11}
Cieux, es-sieu,   heavens, axle-[tree.
see ēū, a see ēū.

⁸ ^{7 11}
O-di-eux,   odious.
ŏ dee ēū.

^{7 11} ^{7 11}
vieux, mieux,   old, better.
vee ēū, mee ēū.

⁵ ¹³ ^{7 11}
pré-ten-ti-eux,   pretentious.
pra tăn see ēū.

^{1 7} ⁸ ^{1 7 11}
a-ïeul, ca-ïeux,   grandfather, [cloves.
ă yuhl, kă yēū.

¹⁴ ⁵ ⁷ ⁸
in-fé-ri-eur,   inferior.
ĭn fa ree uhr.

^{17 7 11} ⁴ ¹³
joy-eu-se-ment,   joyfully.
zhweh yēūz' măn.

⁷ ¹¹ ⁴ ¹³
pi-eu-se-ment,   piously.
pee ēūz' măn.

¹ ⁶ ^{7 8}
la fray-eur,   the fright.
lă freh yuhr.

¹⁶ ⁴ ⁷ ⁸
un re-li-eur,   a bookbinder.
ŭn r'lee uhr.

ă, as; ah, āh, father; uh, ermine; ĕ or ', move; a, late; eh, met; ēh, there; ee, police; ŏ, nor; o, also; ō, no; ŭ, constitution; ēū, first; oo, too; ān, want; ĭn, Yankee; ōn, don't; ŭn, grunt; weh, wear; wah, water; ḡ, go; zh, glazier; ḡn, singing; ȳ, yes.

DIPHTHONGS.

THEORY AND PRACTICE.

175. **io** is a diphthong in **pioche, séméiologie** and their derivatives only.

176. **ïo, yau,** and **yo** are always diphthongs: **iau** always forms a diæresis:—

Ba-ïo-que, bă yŏk'.	baıocco.	Clay-on-na-ge, kleh yŏ năzh'.	basket-work.
tuy-au, a-loy-au, tü ee yo, ă lweh yo.	pipe, sirloin.	myo-pe, meeŏp'.	short-sighted.

177. **ion** forms a diphthong, but only in verbs whose infinitive does not terminate in **ier**. **ri-ons**, from *rire*, has also two syllables. (See § 162.)

Nous a-vions, noo ză vee ōn.	we had.	Nous di-sions, noo dee zee ōn.	we said.

178. **yon** is always a diphthong,— **cray-on, ploy-ons**.

179. **iou** and **you**, little used, form always a diphthong.

Le bi-niou, voy-ou, l' bee nee oo, vweh yoo.	[street boy. the bagpipe,	Piou-piou, you-you, pee oo pee oo, yoo yoo.	[yawl. recruit,
chiour-me, shee oorm'.	convict-gang.	Mon-tes-quiou, mōn tas kee oo.	Montesquiou.

180. **yu** is a diphthong,— **ba-lay-u-re**.

181. **oa** is always a diphthong,— **joail-le-rie, Roan-ne**.

Obs.—In all the diphthongs beginning with **o**, this letter sounds very nearly like **oo** in *too*.

182. **oe** is a diphthong in **moelle** and its derivatives only.

183. **oè** forms a diphthong in **cacatoès** only; but **oê** is always a diphthong, and is pronounced *oua*:—

Poê-le, poo ăhl'.	stove.	Poê-lon, poo ăh lōn.	sauce-pan.
poê-lier, poo ăh lee a.	stove-maker.	poê-le, poo ehl'.	pall.

184. **oi** and **oy** are always diphthongs. **oi** is, however, pronounced **o** in **oignon, encoignure, poignet, poignard, moignon**. (See § 99.)

ă, as; ah, ăh, father; uh, ermine; ĕ or ', move; a, late; eh, met; ĕh, there; ee, police; ŏ, nor; o, also; ō, no; ŭ, constitution; ēū, first; oo, too; ān, want; īn, Yankee; ōn, don't; ūn, grunt; weh, wear; wah, water; ğ, go; zh, glazier; ḡn, singing; ȳ, yes.

THEORY AND PRACTICE.

185. oin is always a diphthong:—

Du ben-join,   some benzine.
dü bïn zhooïn.

loin-tain   far away.
looïn tïn.

U-ne join-tu-re,   a joint.
ün' zhooïn tür'.

a-moin-drir,   to diminish.
ă mooïn dreer.

186. oua is diphthong, but only in **pouah! écouane, bivouac, gouache**, and in their derivatives. In **ouate** it is pronounced **ouè**,— **ouète, ouèter**.

187. oue is diphthong in **ouest, couette, fouet**, and derivatives only. **oué** always forms a diæresis:—

Ouest, fouet,   west, whip.
oo ehst, foo eh.

Lou-é, jou-é,   praised, played.
loo a, zhoo a.

188. ouai forms a diphthong in the exclamation **ouais!** only.

189. oui is diphthong in the two following words and derivatives.

Oui, cam-bouis, yes, cart-grease.
oo ee, kän boo ee.

Cam-boui-sé,   greased.
kän boo ee za.

190. ouan is diphthong in **rouan** only.

191. ouen is a diphthong, but only in **couenne** and **rouenneries**:—

Un che-val rouan, a roan horse.
ün sh' văl roo än.

Couen-neux,   buffy.
koo a neü.

rouen-ne-ries, printed cottons.
roo a n'ree.

192. ouin is always a diphthong:—

Mar-souin,   porpoise.
măr soo ïn.

tin-touin,   tingling.
tïn too ïn.

Ba-ra-gouin,   gibberish.
bă ră goo ïn.

pin-gouin,   penguin.
pïn goo ïn.

ă, as; ah, âh, father; uh, ermine; ĕ or ', move; a, late; eh, met; eh, there; ee, police; ŏ, nor; o, also; ō, no; ŭ, constitution; eū, first; oo, too; än, want; ïn, Yankee; ōn, don't; ün, grunt; weh, wear; wah, water; ḡ, go; zh, glazier; ḡn, singing; ȳ, yes.

DIPHTHONGS.

THEORY AND PRACTICE.

193. There are only five diphthongs which begin with **u**; viz., **ua, ue, ui, uin, uy**.

194. ua is a diphthong only in the following words, in which it is pronounced *oua:* —

<pre>
  1   5 12 2   8 12 2   4   12 1   12 1
A-dé-quat.   Lo-qua-ce.   Quam-quam.
  ă da koo ah.   lŏ   koo ahs'.   koo ăm koo ăm.

  1   12 2   7   8 12 2   7 5   12 1   7   7
al-gua-zil.   lo-qua-ci-té.   quar-ti-di.
  ăl ḡoo ah zeel.   lŏ koo ah see ta.   koo ahr tee dee.

  1   12 2   6   4   1   1   12 13   4   12 1   7 4
a-qua-rel-le.   pa-ra-guan-te.   quar-ti-le.
  ă koo ah rehl'.   pă ră goo ănt'.   koo ahr teel'.

  1   12 2   7 14   12 2   1   5   6   4 12 1   9
a-qua-ri-en.   qua-dra-gé-nai-re.   quar-to.
  ă koo ah ree ĭn.   koo ah dră zha nehr'.   koo ahr to.

  1   12 2   14   4   12 2   1   5 7 1 12 1
a-qua-tin-te.   qua-dra-gé-si-mal.   quartz (and deriv.).
  ă koo ah tĭnt'.   koo ah dră zha zee măl. koo ahrts.

  1   12 2   7   4   12 2   13 10   6 4 12 2   6
a-qua-ti-que.   qua-dran-gu-lai-re.   qua-ter.
  ă koo ah teek'.   koo ah drăn ḡu lehr'.   koo ah tehr.

  8   7 12 2   7   12 2   1   12 2   10 8
col-li-qua-tif.   qua-drat.   qua-tu-or.
  kŏl lee koo ah teef.   koo ah dră.   koo ah tŭ ŏr.

  8   7 12 2   7 15   12 2   1   7   4   10 14 12 2   5   7   1
col-li-qua-tion   qua-dra-tri-ce.   quin-qua-gé-si-mal.
  kŏl lee koo ah see ŏn. koo   ah dră trees'.   kŭ ĭn koo ah zha zee măl.

  5   12 2   7   7   12 2   1 10   4   10 14 12 2   5   7   4
é-qua-ni-mi-té.   qua-dra-tu-re.   quin-qua-gé-si-me.
  a koo ah nee mee ta.   koo ah dră tŭr'.   kŭ ĭn koo ah zha zeem'.

  5   12 2   8   12 2   7   7   4   12 2   4
é-qua-teur.   qua-dri-fi-de.   squa-le.
  a koo ah tuhr.   koo ah dree feed'.   skoo ahl'.

  5   12 2   7 15   12 2   7   4   12 2   4
é-qua-tion.   qua-dri-ge.   squa-me.
  a koo ah see ŏn.   koo ah dreezh'.   skooahm'.

  5   5   12 2   10   12 2   7 1   6   4   12 2   4
e-xé-qua-tur.   qua-dri-la-tè-re.   squa-re.
  a ḡza koo ah tŭr.   koo ah dree lă tehr'.   skooahr.

 12 2   4   12   4   12 2   7   9   4   10   14 12 2
Gua-de-lou-pe.   qua-dri-no-me.   su-blin-gual.
  ḡoo ah d'loop'.   koo ah dree nom'.   sŭ blĭn goo ăl.

 12 2   9   12 2   10   1   4   12 2   5   1   1
gua-no.   qua-dru-ma-ne.   Gua-te-ma-la.
  ḡoo ah no.   koo ah drŭ măn'.   ḡoo ăh ta mă lă.

 14 12 2   12 2   10   4   12 2   1 12 7
lin-gual.   qua-dru-ple.   Guar-da-ful.
  lĭn ḡoo ăl.   koo ah drŭpl'.   ḡoo ăhr dă foo ee.

  7 12 2   7 15   12 2   4   12 2   1   7   7
li-qua-tion.   qua-kre.   Gua-dal-qui-vir.
  lee koo ah see ŏn.   koo ahkr'.   ḡoo ăh dăl kee veer.
</pre>

THEORY AND PRACTICE.

195. ue and **ué** are diphthongs in the following words only:—

5 10 6 4 é-cuel-le. a kü ehl'.	5 10 6 4 é-ques-tre. a kü ehstr'.	10 6 3 ques-teur. kü ehs tuhr.
5 10 5 5 é-cuel-lée. a kü a la.	7 10 5 1 7 15 li-qué-fao-tion. lee kü a fåk see ōn.	6 10 4 ques-tu-re. kü ehs tür'.

196. ui is a diphthong, except in the following words:—

1 10 7 5 A-cu-i-té. ă kü ee ta.	15 10 7 4 [der.] Con-gru-is-me (and kōn grü eesm'.	10 7 7 4 Dru-i-di-que. drü ee deek'.
13 7 10 7 5 am-bi-gu-i-té. ān bee gü ee ta.	15 10 7 4 con-gru-is-te. kōn grü eest'.	10 7 7 4 dru-i-dis-me. drü ee deesm'.
10 7 4 bru-i-ne. brü een'.	15 7 10 7 5 con-ti-gu-i-té. kōn tee gü ee ta.	1 10 7 4 fa-tu-is-me. fă tü eesm'.
10 7 5 bru-i-ner. brü ee na.	5 7 10 7 5 e-xi-gu-i-té. a gzee gü ee ta.	1 10 7 5 fa-tu-i-té. fă tü eest'.
10 7 11 bru-i-neux. brü ee neü.	15 7 10 7 5 con-ti-nu-i-té. kōn tee nü ee ta.	20 7 7 4 su-i-ci-de. sü ee seed'.
10 7 4 bru-i-re. brü eer'.	10 7 4 dru-i-de. drü eed'.	10 7 7 5 su-i-ci-der. sü ee see da.
10 7 4 13 bru-is-se-ment. brü ees' mān.	10 7 6 4 dru-i-des-se. drü ee dehs'.	

197. u after **g** and **q** is generally an orthographic letter, and as such silent: therefore it does not combine with the following vowel to form a diphthong, except in the following words, in which the u retains its full value as a vowel-letter:

5 10 7 4 Ai-guil-le (and der.). a güeeyě.	10 7 1 Gui-sard. gü ee zăr.	15 10 7 8 4 On-gui-for-me. ōn güee förm'.
5 10 7 15 Ai-guil-lon (p. n.). a gü ee yōn.	7 5 14 10 7 4 i-nex-tin-gui-ble. ee na ks tīn güeebl'	13 10 7 7 5 [der.) san-gui-fi-er (and sān güee fee a.
5 10 7 5 ai-gui-ser (and der.). a gü ee za.	14 10 7 1 in-gui-nal. īn güee năl.	15 10 7 6 4 un-gui-fè-re. ōn güee fehr'
15 13 10 7 7 5 con-san-gui-ni-té. kōn sān güee nee ta.	14 10 7 4 lin-guis-te. līn gü eest'.	15 10 7 un-guis. ōn gü ees.
10 7 4 Gui-de (p. n.). gü eed'.	14 10 7 7 4 lin-guis-ti-que. līn güees teek'.	
10 7 4 Gui-se (p. n.). gü eez'.	15 10 7 10 5 on-gui-cu-lé. ōn gü ee kü la.	

DIPHTHONGS. 71

THEORY AND PRACTICE.

198. **ui** forms also a diphthong in the following words:—

5 7 10 7 8	10 7 10	10 7 7 10
De-li-qui-um.	Qui-bus.	Qui-ri-nus.
da lee kü ee ŏm.	kü ee büs.	kü ee ree nüs.
5 10 7 13 4	10 7 7 5	10 7 7 6 4
é-qui-an-gle.	quid-di-té.	qui-ri-tai-re.
a kü ee āṅgl'.	kü eed dee ta.	kü ee ree tehr'.
5 10 7 7 5 13	10 7 5 13	10 7 10
é-qui-dif-fé-rent.	qui-es-cent.	qui-tus.
a kü ee dee fa rāṅ.	kü ee a sāṅ.	kü ee tüs.
5 10 7 7 13	10 7 6	5 10 7 1 6 4
é-qui-dis-tant.	qui-et.	ses-qui-al-tè-re.
a kü ee dees tāṅ.	kü ee eh.	sas kü ee ăl tehr'.
5 10 7 1 6 4	10 7 5 7 4	5 10 7 5 1
é-qui-la-tè-re.	qui-é-tis-me.	ses-qui-pé-dal.
a kü ee lă tehr'.	kü ee a teesm'.	sas kü ee pa dăl.
5 10 7 1 5 1	10 7 5 7 4	5 10 7 10 10 4
é-qui-la-té-ral.	qui-é-tis-te.	ses-qui-sul-fu-re.
a kü ee lă ta răl.	kü ee a teest'.	sas kü ee stil fūr'.
5 10 7 3 7 15	10 7 6 4	(and the other comp.
é-qui-ta-ti-on.	qui-nai-re.	of **sesqui.**)
a kü ee tah see ōṅ.	kǜee nehr'.	
1 10 7 1	10 7 7 1	10 7 10 7 4
a-qui-a.	qui-ri-nal.	u-bi-quis-te.
ă kü ee ă.	kü ee ree năl.	ü bee kü eest'.

199. **uy**, used at the end of proper names only, is a diphthong,— le **Puy**, **Dupuy**, &c.

200. When this group of vowels is followed by another vowel in the body of a word, it always forms two diphthongs in connection with that vowel (see pp. 44, 45), except, of course, when y is followed by a *silent* e.

201. **uin** is a diphthong only in—

10 14	10 14 10 5 1	10 14 7 7
Juin.	Quin-quen-nal.	Quin-ti-di.
zhü īṅ.	kü īṅ kü a năl.	kü īṅ tee dee.
10 14 5 1 9 4	10 14 10 5 7 8	10 14 7 4
quin-dé-ca-go-ne.	quin-quen-nium.	quin-ti-le.
kü īṅ da kă gōn'.	kü īṅ kü a nee ŏm.	kü īṅ teel'.
10 14 5 6 7	70 14 10 6 4	10 14 7 7 14
quin-dé-cem-virs.	quin-quer-ce.	Quin-ti-li-en.
kü īṅ da sehm veer.	kü īṅ kü ehrs'.	kü īṅ tee lee īṅ.
10 14 12 3 5 7 1	10 14 10 5 6 4	10 14 10 4 [der.]
quin-qua-gé-si-mal.	quin-qué-rê-me.	quin-tu-ple (and
kü īṅ koo ah zha zee măl.	kü īṅ kü a rêhm'.	kü īṅ tüpl'.
10 14 12 3 5 7 4	10 14 6 9	
quin-qua-gé-si-me.	quin-tet-to.	
kü īṅ koo ah zha zeem'.	kü īṅ teht to.	

THEORY.

THIRTIETH LESSON. *Trentième leçon.*

CONSONANTS.

202. GENERAL OBSERVATIONS. — Initial consonants are ALWAYS SOUNDED in French; and, when several consonants begin a word, they are *all* pronounced. Even in words beginning with **sce, sci,** or **scy,** the **s,** which is said to be alone sounded, is certainly much strengthened by its association with the **c.**

When two or more words are intimately connected in sense, no solution of continuity in the flow of the voice should occur, and the words must be uttered one after another in one continuous stream, as if they formed but one long word divided into as many syllables as there are vowel-sounds in the whole; therefore, when the first word ends with a consonant and the next begins with a vowel, the final consonant of the first word, which otherwise would be silent, is carried to the second word, with which it is fully sounded, becoming, *de facto,* the initial letter of that word.

We have another and more striking illustration of this resumption of sound by consonant letters, in the case of suffixes, or letters added, for whatever object, to some words. For instance, in **doigt, grand, vingt, petit,** &c., the final **t** or **d** is silent; but in **doigtier, grandeur, vingtième, petitesse,** &c., it is fully sounded, and begins the syllable.

The shortest pause, whether indicated by the punctuation, or not indicated at all, naturally prevents the linking of words together.

THEORY.

CONSONANTS (continued).

GENERAL OBSERVATIONS. — The connection does not take place when it might unpleasantly affect the ear. In familiar conversation, words are more seldom joined together than in serious reading or speaking.

When a consonant is doubled, the second as a general rule is the only one that is sounded; but, in words beginning with **ill, imm, inn, irr, iss,** the two consonants are sounded when the particles **il, im, in, ir, is,** have a negative force.

The addition of an **s,** mark of the plural, does not alter the pronunciation of a word, except in monosyllables which contain no other vowel than **e.** The added **s** lengthens the sound of the syllable.

203. CLASSIFICATION OF THE CONSONANTS. — As the different consonants are respectively produced by the special action of different organs of speech, they have been divided into classes accordingly, and each class designated from the name of the organ which seems to contribute more particularly to the formation of the consonants composing it. Thus we call —

LABIAL, those which are formed by the motion of the lips, — **b, p, f, v, m.**

DENTAL (called also SIBILANT), those which cannot be emitted without the help of the teeth, — **c, ch, s, z.**

LINGUAL, those to the formation of which the tongue contributes more particularly, — **d, l, n, r, t.**

PALATAL, those whose sound is (or seems to be) produced by a motion, or pressing, of the tongue against the palate, — **g, j, c, k, q.**

NASAL, those which are pronounced in part through the nose, — **m, n, gn.**

LIQUID, those which, being joined to another letter, are pronounced easily and smoothly, — **l, r, gn.** The two nasal, **m, n,** may be classed also with the liquid.

THEORY.

CONSONANTS (*continued*).

204. COGNATES. — By comparing certain articulations, it has been found that there is an analogy between them, and that they differ only by greater or less intensity of sound; in consequence of which they have been divided into two classes, and arranged, as they correspond to one another, in couples.

1°. The weak, or whispered, **b, d, g, j, v, z.**
2°. The strong, or spoken, **p, t, c, k, ch, f, g** hard, **s.**

And those letters whose elements are produced by the same organs, in a similar manner, are called *cognates;* as d and t, b and p, f and v, &c.

The following comparison will show how slight is the difference, and how marked is the analogy, between the weak and the strong consonants: —

WEAK CONS.	STRONG CONS.	WEAK CONS.	STRONG CONS.
B.	*P.*	*V.*	*F.*
Bain.	Pain.	Vain.	Faim.
baquet.	paquet.	valoir.	falloir.
beau.	peau.	vanner.	faner.
bercer.	percer.	vaste.	faste.
bois.	pois.	vendre.	fendre.
		viole.	fiole.
J.	*Ch.*		
Jante.	Chante.	*G.*	*C. Q.*
japon.	chapon.	Gaze.	Case.
jarretière.	charretière.	glace.	classe.
jatte.	chatte.	grosse.	crosse.
joie.	choix.	gant.	quand.
D.	*T.*	*Z.*	*S. C.*
Dancer.	Tancer.	Zèle.	Selle.
dard.	tard.	zone.	sonne.
oge.	toge.	zain.	saint.
	tonner.	zinc.	cinq.

THEORY.

CONSONANTS *(continued).*

205. GENERAL REMARKS. — It is a general law of euphony that consonants should be preceded by those of their own kind; *i.e.*, weak consonants call for weak consonant sounds, and strong consonants for strong sounds. For instance, **abstenir, subsister, obtenir, &c.**, are pronounced *apstenir, subzister, optenir,* &c. Thus we see that cognates readily exchange for each other; and, in many instances, the interchange is not only authorized, but obligatory, as the only correct pronunciation.

Each consonant ought to have only one sound, indicated by one character (or letter) only, and that character ought to be incommunicable to any other sound. But, as it happens that in French, as well as in other languages, the same characters represent several sounds, or that different characters are used to represent the same sound, we call natural, or proper, that sound which the consonant habitually represents, and accidental that which it receives accidentally from its position.

206. LONG AND SHORT CONSONANTS. — The explosive b, c, d, g, k, p, q, t, v, are short; the others, generally long. In the expression of strong passion, there is nothing more effective than dwelling particularly upon the consonant sounds. In conversation, long consonants are seldom resorted to, except in the case of considerable emphasis or animation.

THEORY.

THIRTY-FIRST LESSON. *Trente et unième leçon.*

CONSONANT B.

207. Grammarians recognize only one sound of the letter b; but it really has two, — 1°. The natural sound *buh*, the same as in English **bad, mob, elbow**; 2°. The accidental sound *puh*. b is therefore called *buh* and *puh*.

208. As we have already seen, **b** readily permutes with its cognate p, especially before the strong consonant **t**; and also, but not quite so strongly, before **s**. **Subterfuge, obtempérer, s'abstenir, substantif, absence, obscurité,** &c., are pronounced as if written *supterfuge, optempérer, s'apstenir, supstantif, apsence, opscurité,* &c.

209. b is silent before **v**: **Fabvier, Lefebvre,** pronounced *Favié, Lefèvre;* also in **plomb, aplomb, surplomb, Doubs,** and **Christophe Colomb.**

210. The two **b**'s are sounded in **Abbeville, abbatial, gibbeux,** and **gibbosité.**

C.

211. This consonant has three sounds, — the proper sound *kuh*, and the accidental sounds *suh* and *guh*.

212. c final is sounded, except in the words of which a list is given on the opposite page.

213. In the termination of **aspect, circonspect, instinct, respect,** and **suspect,** the c is generally heard in the singular; and the t is silent; but in the plural the c and the t are both mute.

214. **Anspect** and **district** sound the c, both in the singular and in the plural. The t remains silent. In **succint,** the t alone is pronounced.

215. c, which is silent in **marc,** *residuum,* is fully sounded in **Marc,** proper name.

PRACTICE.

THIRTIETH EXERCISE. *Trentième exercice.*

[Jacob.
Le plomb, Ja-cob, the lead,
l' plŏn̄, zhah kŏb,

[wind.
un rumb de vent, a rhumb of
ŭn rŏn̄b duh vān̄.

Au-reng-Zeb, Aureng-Zebe.
ŏ rān̄g zehb.

le ra-doub, the refitting of ships.
l' ră doob.

Ac-croc, a-jonc, rent, sea-rush.
ă kro, ă zhon.

arc-bou-tant, arch-butment.
ăr boo tān̄.

arc-bou-ter, to buttress.
ăr boo ta.

arc-dou-bleau, joist.
ăr doo blo.

[shave.
banc, bec-d'â-ne, bench, spoke-
bān̄, ba dâhn.

blanc, broc, white, jug.
blān̄, bro.

ca-out-chouc, india-rubber.
kă oot shoo.

[tion of quinces.
clerc, co-ti-gnac, clerk, confec-
klehr, kŏ tee ḡnă.

[hook, swindler.
cric, croc, es-croc, screw-jack,
kree, kro, as kro.

es-to-mac, flanc, stomach, side.
as tŏ mă, flān̄.

[then?
il a donc fi-ni? he has finished,
eel ă dōn̄ fee nee.

Franc, jonc, sincere, reed.
frān̄, zhōn̄.

lacs, marc, string, residuum.
lă, măr.

[almanac.
Le-clerc, al-ma-nach, Leclerc,
luh klehr, ăl mă nă.

porc-frais, fresh pork.
pŏr freh.

[arsenic.
rac-croc, ar-se-nic, lucky hit,
ră kro, ăr suh nee.

ta-bac, tronc, tobacco, trunk.
tă bă, trōn̄.

[chess.
jou-er aux é-checs, to play
zhoo a o za sheh.

[thou vanquishest.
je vaincs, tu vaincs, I vanquish,
zh' vin̄, tŭ vin̄.

[St. Mark.
il vainc, St. Marc, he vanquishes,
eel vin̄, sin̄ măr.

l'ins-tinct, the instinct.
lin̄s tin̄.

[concise.
l'a-mict, suc-cinct, the amice,
lă mee, sŭk sin̄t.

ă, as; ah, âh, father; uh, ermine; ĕ or ', move; a, late; eh, met; ēh, there; ee, police; ŏ, nor; o, also; ō, no; ŭ, constitution; ēū, first; oo, too; ān̄, want; īn̄, Yankee; ōn̄, don't; ūn̄, grunt; weh, **wear**; wah, **water**; ḡ, go; zh, glazier; ḡn, singing; ȳ, yes.

THEORY.

CONSONANT C (*continued*).

216. In **porc**, the c is silent, except when **porc** is used figuratively in the sense of glutton:

[he feeds himself. Look at him! What a glutton! **Il se gave, il s'emplit. Regarde-le! le porc!** He stuffs himself,
eel suh gäv', eel sān plee.   ruhgärd' luh, luh pork.

217. In **échecs**, *chess*, the c is silent; but in **échec**, meaning repulse, check, defeat, the c is fully sounded. It is also distinctly heard in **échec et mat**, *checkmate*.

218. In **Saint Marc**, the c is silent, even before a vowel.

219. **ct** at the end of words are both sounded, except in **aspect, circonspect, instinct, respect, suspect**, and **amict**. In **succinct**, the t alone is pronounced. (See § 214.)

220. **Violoncelle** and **vermicelle** are now regularly pronounced *violon(s)elle, vermi(s)elle*.

221. In a few expressions, such as those given on the page opposite, the final c of a few words, in which it is ordinarily silent, resumes its full sound as **k** in *key*.

222. The c of the conjunction **donc**, *therefore* (the *ergo* of the Latin), is sounded, —

1°. Before a vowel or a silent **h**;
2°. When **donc** is placed at the beginning of a proposition;
3°. In sentences expressing passion, indignation, anger, &c.;
    ex.: —

    Vous voilà donc enfin arrivé.
    Elle refuse, donc je pars.
    Vous prétendez donc me dicter des lois!

Everywhere else the c of **donc** is silent.

223. When c is doubled, and the second is followed by **e** or **i**, so that it takes the s-sound, this makes the two c's virtually different letters, and naturally both must be sounded. The first c keeps the proper sound (as **k** in *key*): the second takes the sound *suh* (as **s** in *so*).

PRACTICE.

THIRTY-FIRST EXERCISE. *Trente et unième exercice.*

Il a reçu un fameux écheo,   He was severely repulsed.
eel ă r'sŭ   ŭn̄ fă meū za shehk.

Vous avez trop de respect humain, You fear the world too much.
voo ză va   trŏ   d'rehs pehk ŭ min̄.

Je l'ai fait échec et mat,   I checkmated him.
zh' la feh a shehk a măt.

Votre cousin Marc ne vient pas, Your cousin Mark does not come.
vŏtr'   koo zin̄ mărk nuh vee in̄ pah.

C'est un marchand de bric-à-brac, He is a dealer in old stores.
seh tŭn̄ măr shau̅   d' breek ă brăk.

                                                  [dealing in that affair.
Il y a du micmac dans cette affaire, There is some underhand
eel ee ă dŭ meek măk dan̄   seht ă fehr'.

                                                  [every evening.
Nous jouions au trictrac tous les soirs. We played backgammon
noo   zhoo yon̄ zo   treek trăk too   la swehr.

                                                  [of the mill?
Entendez-vous le tic-tac du moulin? Do you hear the click-clack
an̄ tan̄ da   voo   l' teek tăk dŭ moo lin̄.

                                                  [less fellow.
Votre neveu est un franc étourdi, Your nephew is a thought-
vŏtr'   nuh veū eh tŭn̄ fran̄ ka toor dee.

                               [goes from one extreme to the other.
Cet avocat passe toujours du blanc au noir, That lawyer always
seht ă vŏ kă   pahs' too zhoor dŭ   blan̄   ko nwehr.

                               [count of your receipts and expenditures.
Nous compterons de clerc à maître, We shall give an exact ac-
noo   kōn̄ tron̄   d' klehrk ă mehtr'.

                                                 [onomatopœia.
Cric-crac est une onomatopée familière, Cric-crac is a familiar
keek krăk en tŭn' ŏ nŏ mă tŏ pa fă mee lee ehr'.

Le porc-épic dresse ses piquants, The porcupine erects his quills.
l'   pŏr ka peek drehs'   sa pee kan̄.

Il lui a donné un croc en jambe, He tripped him up.
eel lŭ ee ă dŏna   ŭn̄ krŏk an̄ zhan̄b'.

ă, as; ah, âh, father; uh, ermine; ŏ or ', move; a, late; eh, met;
ēh, there; ee, police; ŏ, nor; o, also; ō, no; ŭ, constitution;
eū, first; oo, too; an̄, want; in̄, Yankee; ōn̄, don't; ŭn̄,
grunt; weh, **wear**; wah, **water**; ğ, go; zh, glazier; g̃n, singing; y̆, yes.

THEORY.

THIRTY-SECOND LESSON. *Trente-deuxième leçon.*

CONSONANT *C* (*continued*).

224. In the five following words the two **c**'s are pronounced as double **k**, — **peccable, peccadille, peccata, peccant, peccavi.**

225. **c** has the accidental sound *guh* (as **g** in *go*) in the following words and in their derivatives:

Second, fécond, Czar, [fruitful, Czar, second,	**Reine-claude,** green-gage.
s'gōn, fă gōn, gzăr.	rāhn' glōd'.

226. The combination **sc**, at the beginning of words, and followed by **e, i,** or **y**, is sounded as in the English word *science.* Both the **s** and **c** are pronounced; or, as the **s** and the **c** have here the same sound, it would be more correct to say that the **s** is not only fully sounded, but receives additional strength from its association with the **c**, which might be called silent.

227. **c**, as well as **p** and **s**, between two consonants, forms a syllable with the first; *ex.*: **fonc-tion, domp-teur, superstitiéux.**

COMBINATION *CH.*

228. In words purely French and in those which come from the Latin, the combination **ch**, followed by a vowel, is pronounced as in English in **machine**; and, in spelling for pronunciation, is called *shuh.*

OBS. — In this case, the **h** after **c** is merely an auxiliary letter; and, in connection with the **c**, becomes the symbol of the strong articulation whose weak counterpart is represented by the letter **j**. The **h**, therefore, does not represent an aspirate in the primitive word.

229. But in words of foreign origin, mostly from the Greek, and the other languages of the East, whose syllable, to which **ch** belongs, *has been preserved in its primitive orthography,* the **ch** has retained its hard sound, as **k** in *key,* and is called *kuh.*

OBS. — Here the **h** is simply an etymological letter: it serves only to indicate that the radical words had an **h** aspirate, the sign of which has been retained in the derivatives.

PRACTICE.

THIRTY-SECOND EXERCISE. *Trente-deuxième exercice.*

CH HARD, AS K IN KEY.

Archéologique,	archeological.	**Gutta-percha,**	gutta-percha.
ăr ka ŏ lŏ zheek'.		gŭ tă pehr kă.	
anachorète,	hermit.		[(metal).
ă nă kŏ rĕht'.		**du melchior,**	some melchior
Cham,	Ham.	dŭ mehl kee or.	
kăm.		**l'orchestre,**	the orchestra.
chiste,	cyst.	l'ŏr kehstr'.	
keest'.			[nezzar.
	[cer.	**Nabuchodonozor,**	Nebuchad-
un chiromancien,	a chiroman-	nă bŭ kŏ dŏ nŏ zŏr.	
ūn kee rŏ mān see īn.			[bees.
		les Machabées,	the Macca-
le chélone,	the tortoise-flower.	la mă kă ba.	
luh ka lŏn'.		**Tychobrahé,**	Tycho-Brahe.
Chanaan,	Canaan.	tee ko bră a.	
kă nă ān.		**Michel-Ange,**	Michael Angelo.
		mee kehl ānzh'.	
le chœur,	the choir.	**un écho,**	an echo.
l' kuhr.		ūn na ko.	
scholaire,	academic.	**Machiavel,**	Machiavel.
skŏ lehr'.		mă kee ă vehl.	
Civita-Vecchia,	Civita-Vecchia.	**l'eucharistie,**	the Eucharist.
see vee tă vehk kee ă.		lēu kă rees tee.	
de la malachite,	some malachite.	**un archange,**	an archangel.
d' lă mă lă keet.		ūn năr kānzh'.	
inchoatif,	inceptive.	**fuchsia,**	fuchsia.
īn kŏ ă teef.		fŭk see ă.	

ă, as; ah, âh, father; uh, ermine; ĕ or ', move; a, late; eh, met; ēh, there; ee, police; ŏ, nor; o, also; ō, no; ŭ, constitution; ēu, first; oo, too; ān, want; īn, Yankee; ōn, don't; ūn, grunt; weh, **wear**; wah, **water**; ḡ, go; zh, glazier; ḡn, singing; ȳ, yes.

THEORY.

THIRTY-THIRD LESSON. *Trente-troisième leçon.*

COMBINATION *CH (continued).*

230. **Machiavélique, archevêque, archevêché,** and **patriarche** have the **ch** soft, as in *machine*. The reason for this apparent irregularity lies in the fact that the adjective *machiavélique* is of French formation, while **Machiavel** is Italian. **Archiépiscopal** has come to us with its Eastern prefix *archi*, but **archevêque** is French. **Patriarchal** pronounces a pure Latin finale (*chalis*): **patriarche** has a French termination.

231. Several words in the same category, having become more common than others, have insensibly lost their original pronunciation (**ch** hard), and have taken that of the French **ch** (soft); such as, **archidiacre, chimie, architecte, chirurgien, Achille, Joachim, archiprêtre, chérubin, tachygraphie, Zachée, Achéron,** &c.

232. **Chélidoine,** *celandine,* has the **ch** hard or soft at the option of the speaker. **Gutta-percha** is generally pronounced *goutta-peurtsha,* but many have gallicized it into **guta-perka.** La cachucha is pronounced *katshoutsha.*

233. **ch** preceded by **c,** or followed by a consonant, or terminating a word, is pronounced *kuh* (as **k** in *key*). However **ch** is silent in **almanach,** and is sounded as **g** hard in *drachme:*

[roar, the log-line.	[chante, Chloe.
Un bacchanal, le loch, an up-	Une bacchante, Chloé, a bac-
ūn bă kă năl, luh lŏk.	tin' bă kānt', klŏa.

In the combination **cht,** at the end of words, the **t** is silent. The **ch** is, according to rule pronounced as **k** in *key.*

[Utrecht.	
Les yachts, Utrecht, the yachts,	**Maëstricht,** Maestricht.

PRACTICE.

THIRTY-THIRD EXERCISE. *Trente-troisième exercice.*

CH HARD, AS K IN *KEY.*

Catéchumène,	catechumen.	Chorégraphie,	choregraphy
kă ta kŭ mĕhn.		kŏ ra ḡră fee.	
Zacharie,	Zachary.	Pulchérie,	Pulcheria.
ză kă ree.		pŭl ka ree.	
la Chaldée,	Chaldea.	Charybde,	Charybdis.
lă kăl da.		kă reebd'.	

Judith a une chaîne en chrysocale, Judith has a pinchbeck chain.
zhŭ deet ă ŭn' shēhn a͞n kree zŏ kăl'.

Les élèves de l'école polytechnique, The students of the Poly-
la za lĕhv' duh la kŏl' pŏ lee tehk neek'. [technic School.

Donnez-moi un drachme de séné, Give me a drachm of senna.
dŏ na mweh u͞n drăḡm' duh sana.

La chlamyde des Romains, The chlamys of the Romans.
lă klă meed' da rŏ mi͞n.

Le chlore sert à blanchir les toiles, Chlorine serves to bleach linen.
l' klŏr sehr tă bla͞n sheer la twehl'.

Les Israélites sacrifièrent à Moloch, The Israelites sacrificed to
la zeez ră a leet' să kree fee ĕhr tă mŏ lŏk. [Moloch.

Zurich est la patrie de Lavater, Zurich is Lavater's birthplace.
zŭ reek eh lă pă tree d' lă vă tehr.

ă, as; ah, äh, father; uh, ermine; ŏ or ', move; a, late; eh, met; ēh, there; ee, police; ŏ, nor; o, also; ō, no; ŭ, constitution; ēū, first; oo, too; a͞n, want; i͞n, Yankee; o͞n, don't; u͞n, grunt; weh, wear; wah, water; ḡ, go; zh, glazier; ḡn, singing; ȳ, yes.

THEORY.

THIRTY-FOURTH LESSON. *Trente-quatrième leçon.*

CONSONANT D.

234. **d** final is sounded in proper names of foreign origin, and in the words **cid, éphod, sud.**

d final takes accidentally the sound of its cognate **t**: —

1°. In adjectives followed by their substantive, the latter beginning with a vowel or a mute **h**. But the **d** remains silent when the substantive begins with a consonant or an **h** aspirate; also when the adjective is followed by any other word than its substantive.

2°. In verbs, but only before **il, elle, on**.

3°. In **quand**, before a vowel or a mute **h**.

In the termination **dt**, the **d** alone is sounded.

d final is silent in substantives, also in the adjectives **chaud, froid, rond,** and in the adverb **tard**.

But in compound expressions, the **d** of the substantives **pied** and **fond** is fully sounded, except in **pied-à-pied**.

235. The two **d**'s are sounded in the following words only: **addition, additionnel, reddition, adducteur, quiddité.**

CONSONANT F.

236. In **neuf**, **f** assumes the sound of its cognate **v**, but only before a substantive or an adjective beginning with a vowel or a mute **h**. If they begin with a consonant, **f** is silent.

Neuf, used to form complex or compound words, does not sound its **f** before a consonant. **Neuf-Brisack, Neufbourg, Neufchâtel,** neuf cents, &c., are pronounced *Neubrisack, Neubour, Neuchâtel, neu cent,* &c.

Everywhere else, **f** of **neuf** retains its natural sound.

237. **f** is silent in **clef, éteuf, le bœuf-gras, cerf-volant, chef-d'œuvre**; also in the three plural words **œufs, bœufs, nerfs.** In **nerf de bœuf**, singular and plural, the **f** of **nerf** is silent.

In **cerf**, *stag*, the **f** is fully sounded, except when **cerf** is used as a hunting-term.

PRACTICE.

THIRTY-FOURTH EXERCISE. *Trente-quatrième exercice.*

De fond en comble, from top to [bottom.
duh fōñ tāñ kōñbl'.
armé de pied en cap, armed [from top to toe.
ăr ma duh pee a tāñ kăp.
il est grand et beau, he is tall [and handsome.
eel eh grāñ a bo.
Entend-elle? Does she hear?
āñ tāñ tehl'.
le Talmud, the Talmud.
l' tăl mŭd.
un nerf de bœuf, a cow-hide.
ŭñ nehr duh buhf.
j'ai un cerf-volant, I have a kite.
zha ŭñ sehr vŏ lāñ.
une attaque de nerfs, a nervous [attack.
ŭn' ă tăk duh nehr.
le bœuf gras, the fatted (carni- [val) ox.
l' beū grah.
un œuf dur, a boiled egg.
ŭñ nuhf dŭr.
je lui en donne neuf, I give [him nine.
zh' lŭ ee āñ dŏn' nuhf.
le cerf brame, the stag is belling.
l' sehr brăm'.

Il a un pied-à-terre, he has a [temporary lodging.
eel a ŭñ pee a tă tehr'.
il avance pied-à-pied, he ad- [vances step by step.
eel ă vāñs' pee a ă pee a.
un profond abîme, a deep [abyss.
ŭñ prŏ fōñ tă beem'.
profond ou non, deep or not.
prŏ fōñ oo nōñ.
quand elle viendra, when she [comes.
kāñ tehl' vee iñ dră.
le Sund, the Sound.
l' sŭñd.
c'est un chef-d'œuvre, that is a [master-piece.
seh tŭñ sheh duhvr'.
du bœuf frais, some fresh beef.
dŭ buhf freh.
il a dix-neuf ans, he is nineteen [years old.
eel ă deez neū vāñ.
neuf cavaliers, nine horsemen.
nuh kă vă lee a.
un cerf dix cors, a full-grown [stag.
ŭñ sehr dee kŏr.
des bas-reliefs, some bas-reliefs.
da bah r'lee ehf.

ă, as; ah, āh, father; uh, ermine; ŏ or ', move; a, late; eh, met; ēh, there; ee, police; ŏ, nor; o, also; ō, no; ŭ, constitution; eū, first; oo, too; āñ, want; īñ, Yankee; ōñ, don't; ūñ, grunt; weh, wear; wah, water; ğ, go; zh, glazier; gñ, singing; y̆, yes.

THEORY.

THIRTY-FIFTH LESSON. *Trente-cinquième leçon.*

CONSONANT G.

238. **g** final is sounded (as in *go*) in proper names of persons, and in words from foreign languages; also in **zigzag**, and slightly in **joug**.

239. **g** has also the hard sound in **Borghèse, Bergheim, Gessner, Enghien, Gessler**, and generally in proper names of German origin.

240. In **bourg** (final syllable of some proper names of towns and countries), the **g** is silent; but is sounded as **k** in the common noun **bourg**, *market-town;* also in **Bourg en Bresse**.

241. In **long** and **sang** the **g** takes the sound of **k** before a vowel or a silent **h**. In **rang**, the **g** is now silent in all cases, even in poetry. In **orang-outang**, the first **g** is either sounded or silent: the last is silent.

242. In **gangrène** and its derivatives, the **g** initial, which was formerly sounded as **k**, has now resumed its natural sound (as in *go*).

243. **Suggérer** in all its tenses, **suggesté**, and **suggestion** sound the two **g**'s, the first as in *go*, the second as **z** in *glazier*. Everywhere else, when double, the second **g** alone is sounded.

244. In the Italian proper names and words **Castiglione, Cagliostro, Cagliari, imbroglio**, &c., the g-sound is suppressed in French, as it is in Italian; and, by analogy, we drop it also in **de la Seiglière**. **Broglie** is pronounced *broyi*. But in all French words the combined consonants **gl** are both pronounced, and called *gluh*.

245. Concerning **gu**. In the following words and in their derivatives, the **u** is not an orthographic letter; and, consequently, is fully sounded,— **aiguille, exiguïté, sanguification, arguer, unguis, le Guide, aiguiser, linguiste, inextinguible, les Guises, la Guyanne, la Guienne**. (See § 198.) **Guanches** is pronounced *gooansh'*.

PRACTICE.

THIRTY-FIFTH EXERCISE. *Trente-cinquième exercice.*

Un joug affreux, a frightful yoke.
ŭñ zhookă freū.
Borghèse, Borghese.
bŏr ḡehz'.
Gessner, zigzag, Gessner, [zigzag.
ḡehs nehr, zeeḡ zăg.
Gessler, Enghien, Gessler, [Enghien.
ḡehs lehr, āñ ḡiñ.
rang élevé, high rank.
rāñ a l' va.
un long accès, a long attack.
ŭñ lōñ kăk seh.
Saint-Pétersbourg, St. Peters- [burg.
sĭñ pa tehrs boor.
l'aiguilleur, the switcher.
leh ḡü ee yuhr.
un orang-outang, an orang- [outang.
ŭñ nŏ rāñ oo tāñ.
je suggère, I suggest.
zhuh sŭḡ zhĕhr'.
rue Bourg-l'Abbé, Bourg- [l'Abbe Street.
rü boor lăba.
Bourg en Bresse, Bourg in [Bresse.
boor kāñ brehs'.

Cagliostro, Cagliostro.
kă lee os tro.
une suggestion, a suggestion.
ün' sŭḡ zhehs tee ōñ.
un imbroglio, an imbroglio.
ŭñ niñ brŏ lee o. [la Seiglière.
Mlle. de la Seiglière, Mlle. de
măd' mweh zehl' duh lă sa lee ehr'.
le Duc de Broglie, the Duke [de Broglie.
l' dŭk duh brŏ yee.
le Duc de Guise, the Duke de [Guise.
l' dŭk duh ḡü eez'.
le Guide, Guido.
luh ḡü eed'.
la Guienne, Guienne.
lă ḡü ee ehn'.
Augsbourg, Augsburg.
oz boor.
un legs incertain, an uncertain [legacy.
ŭñ leh ziñ sehr tiñ.
nous arguons, we argue.
noo zăr ḡü ōñ.
une aiguière, a ewer.
ün' eh ḡü ee ehr'.

ă, as ; ah, ăh, father ; uh, ermine ; ĕ or ', move ; a, late ; eh, met ;
ĕh, there ; ee, police ; ŏ, nor ; o, also ; ō, no ; ŭ, constitution ;
ēū, first ; oo, too ; āñ, want ; iñ, Yankee ; ōñ, don't ; ūñ,
grunt ; weh, wear ; wah, water ; ḡ, go ; zh, glazier ; ḡñ, singing ; ȳ, yes.

THEORY.

THIRTY-SIXTH LESSON. *Trente-sixième leçon.*

CONSONANT *G (GU continued).*

246. The pronunciation of the **u** of **Guise** is disappearing little by little. In the common nouns **guise** and **guide**, the **u** is, of course, silent. The verb **arguer**, in all its inflections, distinctly sounds the **u**; but the latter is silent in about fifty verbs ending in *guer*.

247. **u** is also silent in **aiguade, aigayer, aiguail**; but in all the other words containing **gua**, the **u** forms a diphthong with the **a**, and therefore retains its full value as a vowel letter. It is evident that, in that class of words, the **u** of **gua** is not an orthographic letter, since the **g** would be hard without it. (See § 194.)

COMBINATION *GN.*

248. **gn** has two sounds:—

1°. The soft or liquid sound, which is the proper sound of the French **gn**, and is identical with the sound represented by **ng** in *singing*. (See § 44.)
2°. The hard sound, which is formed by the two distinct articulations, **guh** (g) and **nuh** (n), so intimately united as to come out in one explosion of the voice.

The hard **gn** sound is limited to words beginning with that combination, and to a few others, and their derivatives, given on the page opposite.

249. The popular appellative **gnaf**, *cobbler*, is the only word that has the initial **gn** soft.

250. The **g** sound is generally suppressed in **magnifique, magnificence, magnifiquement, signet, signifier, Regnard, Compiègne, Régnault, Clugny, Augsbourg, legs.**

PRACTICE.

THIRTY-SIXTH EXERCISE. *Trente-sixième exercice.*

A ma guise,	in my own way.	**Signet,**	pointer (for books).
ă mă ḡeez'.		see neh.	
aiguade,	stream of water.	**cela signifie,**	that signifies.
eh ḡăd'.		s' lă see nee fee.	
un gnaf,	a cobbler.	**Compiègne,**	Compiegne.
ūn ḡnăf.		kōn pee ehn'.	
M. de Clugny,	Mr. de Clugny.	**magnifiquement,**	magnificently.
muh see ēu d' klū nee.		mă nee feek' măn.	

gn hard, as in *ignorant*.

			[nate.
Agnus, agnat,[*]	agnus, collateral.	**Progné, cognat,**	Prognee, cog-
ă ḡnŭs, ă ḡnă.	[ous.	prŏḡna, kŏ ḡnă.	
géognosie, igné,	geognosy, igne-	**diagnostic,**	diagnostic.
zha ŏ ḡno zee, ee ḡna.		dee ă ḡnŏs teek.	
magnificat,	magnificat.	**inexpugnable,**	inexpugnable.
mă ḡnee fee kăt.		ee na ks pü ḡnăbl'.	
stagnant,	stagnant.	**pugnacité,**	combativeness.
stă ḡnān.		pü ḡnă see ta.	
magnat,	magnate.	**régnicole,**	native (law term).
mă ḡnă.	[my.	ra ḡnee kŏl'.	
physiognomonie,	physiogno-	**désignatif,**	designative.
fee zee ŏ ḡnŏ mŏ nee.		da zee ḡnă teef.	
Cavagnari,[*]	Cavagnari.	**M. Savagner,**[*]	Mr. de Savagner.
kă vă nee ă ree.		muh see ēu să vă nee a.	

---

[*] **gn** has even a third sound, very little in use: it introduces the i sound and suppresses the **g,** as in the name *Cavagnari*, of Italian origin, and in *Savagner*, &c.

ă, as; ah, ăh, father; uh, ermine; ĕ or ', move; a, late; eh, met; ēh, there; ee, police; ŏ, nor; o, also; ō, no; ŭ, constitution; ēu, first; oo, too; ān, want; īn, Yankee; ōn, don't; ūn, grunt; weh, wear; wah, water; g, go; zh, glazier; ḡn, singing; ȳ, yes.

THEORY.

THIRTY-SEVENTH LESSON. *Trente-septième leçon*.

CONSONANT *H*.

251. h aspirate gives strength to the following vowel, but the h itself is altogether silent.

252. h initial and aspirate prevents the elision of the final vowel of the preceding word; and, if that word ends with a consonant, the aspirate h prevents the connection between the two words. But if that final consonant be habitually sounded, as c, l, r, &c., it naturally retains its sound before h aspirate, as before all other consonants.

253. h initial is generally aspirate in words implying great moral or physical power or strength, also in words derived from the Greek or some foreign language.

254. h mute, initial or not, is null, and, as far as pronunciation is concerned, altogether useless.

255. h initial is generally mute in words derived from the Latin, as **habile, haleine, heure, huile, huître, hiver,** &c., which come from *habilis, halo, hora, oleum, ostreum, hiems,* &c. However, **héros, hennir, harpie,** and a few others which came originally from the Greek, have the h aspirate.

256. h after a consonant is null; therefore **inhumain, inhérent, exhausser,** &c., are thus divided, — *i-nhu-main, i-nhé-rent, e-xhaus-ser*.

257. Between two vowels, h begins the syllable, — tra-hir co-hue, ba-hut, an-ni-hi-ler, ca-hier, ap-pré-hen-der, co-hor-te, co-hé-sion, bo-hé-mien, sou-hai-ter, pé-ri-hé-lie, &c., — and consequently is aspirate.

258. h, which is aspirate in **héros** (from the Greek), is mute in all its derivatives, the latter being of French formation: —

[the heroine.
Les héros, l'héroïne, the heroes,
la a ro, la ro een'.

Vers héroïques, heroic verses.
vehr za ro eek'.

THEORY AND PRACTICE.

259. **h** initial is generally aspirate in foreign proper names.

OBS.— A singular custom, which prevailed for some time, caused the aspiration of the **h**, in the three expressions, *toile d'Hollande, fromage d'Hollande, eau de la reine d'Hongrie,* to disappear; but, at the present day, all those who pride themselves upon their good speaking always pronounce these expressions with the **h** aspirate.

Dans un fromage de Hollande,   In a Dutch cheese.
daṅ   zuṅ frŏ măzh' duh ŏ lāṅd'.
De l'eau de la reine de Hongrie,   Some Hungary water.
d'   ·l'o   d' lă rĕhn' duh ōṅ grēe.
De la toile de Hollande,   Some Dutch linen.
d'   lă twehl' duh ŏ lāṅd'.

260. The **h** of **Henri** is generally mute in familiar conversation, and aspirate in the elevated, noble style, and high diction:—

Jusqu'à la mort de Henri IV.,   Until the death of Henry IV.
zhūs kă lă mŏr duh āṅ ree kătr'.
[Henry IV.
Vic, compagnon d'armes de Henri IV.,   Vic, companion of
veek, kōṅ pă gnōṅ d' ărm' duh āṅ ree kătr'.
Le cheval d'Henri IV.,   The horse of Henry IV.
luh sh' văl d' āṅ ree kătr'.
Les thèmes d'Henri,   Henry's themes.
la   tĕhm'   d' āṅ ree.

261. The **h** of **la Henriade** is never mute; that of **Henriette**, never aspirate.

262. **h** is mute when it is preceded by a consonant and followed by a vowel; but when the particle **en** is prefixed to a word whose **h** is aspirate, the **h** remains aspirate in the compound, and the particle **en** retains its nasal sound:—

[ness.
Nous enharnachons, we har-   **Il s'enhardit,** he grows bold.
noo zaṅ ăr nă shōṅ.   eel saṅ ăr dee.

PRACTICE.

THIRTY-SEVENTH EXERCISE. *Trente-septième exercice.*

LIST OF THE MOST COMMONLY USED WORDS BEGINNING WITH *H* ASPIRATE.

Ha! hâbler,	ah, ăh blă.		ha! to boast.
la hache,	lă ăsh'.		the axe.
hagard, hai!	ă găr, ăh.		haggard, ha!
la haie, haïe,	lă eh, ă ee.		the hedge, gee-oh!
les haillons,	la ăh yōn.		the rags.
la haine,	lă ăhn'.		hatred.
haïr, la haire,	ă eer, lă ehr.		to hate, the hair-[shirt.
le hâle, haler,	luh ăhl', ăh la.		the sun-burn, to [tow.
une halle,	ūnuh ăl'.		a market.
la hallebarde,	lă ăl' bărd'.		the halberd.
la halte,	lă ălt'.		the halt.
mon hamac,	mōn ă măk.		my hammock.
les hameaux,	la ă mo.		the hamlets.
La hampe,	lă ănp'.		the staff.
la hanche,	lă ănsh'.		the hip.
un hangar,	ūn ăn găr.		a shed.
les hannetons,	la ăn' tōn.		the May-bugs.
happer, hanter,	ă pa, ăn ta.		to snap, to fre-[quent.
une haguenée,	ū nuh ăk' na.		an ambling nag.
le haquet,	luh ă keh.		the dray.
la harangue,	lă ă răng'.		the harangue.
harasser,	ă ră sa.		to harass.
harceler,	ăr suh la.		to harass.
les hardes,	la ărd'.		the clothes.
hardi, le harem,	ăr dee, luh ă rehm.		bold, the harem.
un hareng,	ūn ă răn.		a herring.

ă, as; ah, ăh, father; uh, ermine; ĕ or ', move; a, late; eh, met; ēh, there; ee, police; ŏ, nor; o, also; ō, no; ŭ, constitution; eū, first; oo, too; ăn, want; īn, Yankee; ōn, don't; ūn, grunt; weh, wear; wah, water; ḡ, go; zh, glazier; ḡn, singing; ȳ, yes.

PRACTICE.

Les haricots, *la ă ree ko.*	the beans.
une haridelle, *ŭ nuh ă ree dehl'.*	a jade.
harnacher, *ăr nă sha.*	to harness.
la harpe, *lă ărp'.*	the harp.
une harpie, *ŭ nuh ăr pee.*	a harpy.
les harpons, *la ăr pōn.*	the harpoons.
le hasard, *luh ă zăr.*	the hazard.
hâter, à la hâte, *ăh ta, ă lă ăht'.*	to haste, in a [hurry.
hausser, haute, *o sa, ōt.*	to raise, high.
haut, hâve, *e, ăhv'.*	high, emaciated.
un havre, hé! *ūn ahvr', a.*	a harbor, hey!
hein! héler, *īn, a la.*	what! to hail.
hem! hennir, *ehm, ă neer.*	hem! to neigh.
la Henriade, *lă ān ree ăd'.*	the Henriade.
un hérault, *ūn a ro.*	a herald.
Un pauvre hère, *ūn po vruh ehr.*	a poor wretch.
le hérisson, *luh a ree sōn.*	the hedge-hog.
les hérons, le héros, *la a rōn, luh a ro.*	[the hero. the herons,
heu! heurter, *ēū, uhr ta.*	ay! to knock.
hideux, ho! *ee dēū, ă.*	hideous, ho!
holà! hom! *o lă, om.*	halloa! hem!
un homard, *ūn ŏ măr.*	a lobster.
la honte, le hoquet, *lă ōnt', luh ŏ keh.*	[the hiccough. the shame,
une horde, *ŭ nuh ŏrd'.*	a horde.
un horion, hormi, *ūn o ree ōn, ŏr mee.*	[cepted. a thump, ex-
hors, une hotte, *ŏr, ŭ nuh ŏt'.*	[a basket-funnel. excepted,
du houblon, *dū oo blōn.*	some hops.
de la houille, *d' lă ooy'.*	some coal.

ă, as; ah, äh, father; uh, ermine; ŏ or ', move; a, late; eh, met; ēh, there; ee, police; ŏ, nor; o, also; ō, no; ŭ, constitution; ēū, first; oo, too; ān, want; īn, Yankee; ōn, don't; ūn, grunt; weh, wear; wah, water; ḡ, go; zh, glazier; ḡn, singing; ȳ, yes.

PRACTICE.

La houle,	the surge.	Un Huguenot,	a Huguenot
lă ool'.		ŭn ŭg' no.	
sa houlette,	his shepherd's hook.	le huit,	the eight.
să oo leht'.		luh ŭ eet.	
une houri,	a houri.	une hure,	a head.
ŭ nuh oo ree.		ŭ nuh ŭr'.	
la houssine,	the switch.	hurler,	to howl.
lă oo seen'.		ŭr la.	
du houx,	some holly-wood.	le hussard,	the hussar.
dŭ oo.		luh ŭ săr.	
un chat huant,	a screech-owl.	les huttes,	the huts.
ŭn shă ŭ ăn.		lă ŭt'.	

with their compounds and derivatives.

263. The h of **huit, huitième, huitièmement,** is mute when these words are preceded by *dix, vingt, soixante-dix,* or *quatre-vingt-dix:* —

Dix-huit,	eighteen.	**Vingt-huitième,**	twenty-eighth.
deez tieet.		vĭn tŭ ee tee ehm'.	

Quatre-vingt-dix-huitième, ninety-eighth.
kă truh vĭn dee zŭ ee tee ehm'.

264. h is now mute in the following twelve words: l'hallali, l'hamecon, l'heiduque, poire de bon-henri, l'hernute, hershel, l'hidalgo, l'hiéroglyphe, l'hyène, l'hortensia, l'hospodar, l'hospodarat.

ă, as; ah, äh, father; uh, ermine; ŏ or ', move; a, late; eh, met; ēh, there; ee, police; ŏ, nor; o, also; ō, no; ŭ, constitution; ēŭ, first; oo, too; ān, want; ĭn, Yankee; ōn, don't; ŭn, grunt; weh, wear; wah, water; g, go; zh, glazier; gn, singing; y, yes.

THEORY.

THIRTY-EIGHTH LESSON. *Trente-huitième leçon.*

CONSONANT *H* (*continued*).

265. **Hors de combat.** — The expression *hors du combat* — meaning OUT OF or BEYOND the limits of a particular fight, whether able or not to participate in it — is often, and wrongly, used instead of **hors de combat,** — which means *not in a condition to fight*, because of wounds or for any other cause, and whether on the battle-field or not. Those who adhere to the expression *hors du combat* (in spite of Worcester and Webster, to say nothing of French authority) merely show a deplorable ignorance of the genius of our language. **Esprit de corps, mal de tête,** and a number of other expressions, may be classed in the same category.

266. If we consult a dictionary, — that of the Academy, for instance, — we shall find that all words beginning with **hac, hic, hoc, hou, huc, han, hap, hag, har, has, hat, han, hav,** except *hanebane, harmonie,* and deriv., *hast* and *hastair, haras, harpège, harpéger, haruspice,* and *haussière,* have the **h** aspirate.

267. And all words beginning with **hend, hept, hex, hip, hir, his,** and **hiv,** with the single exception of **hisser,** have the **h** mute.

CONSONANT *J*.

268. **j** never terminates French words. When final in foreign words it is fully sounded.

CONSONANT *K*.

269. **k** is everywhere sounded as in *key*.
270. **c** before **k** is, of course, silent.

THEORY AND PRACTICE.

CONSONANT *L*.

271. l has the natural sound *luh* (as in *level*): —
1°. At the beginning of words.
2°. When single in the middle of words.
3°. When double in the middle of words, provided it is not immediately preceded by i.
4°. After the combination oi, whether the l be final or not.
5°. In the termination il preceded by a consonant.
6°. When final and not preceded by i following another vowel.
7°. In il and ill at the beginning of words.

272. l is silent in **anil, baril, chenil, courtil, coutil, fayols, fraisil, fournil, fusil, fils, gril, faulx, aulx, gentils, nombril, outil, persil, pouls, soûl, sourcil, cul-de-sac,** which are pronounced *ani, bari, cheni, courti, couti, fayo, frési, fourni, fusi, fis, gri, fo, o, genti, nombri, outi, persi, pou, sou, sourci, cu-de-sac.*

Also in a number of proper names; such as **Arnault, Chaulny, Faultrier, Maulny, Paulmier, Lons-le-Saulnier, Dumesnil, Gentil-Bernard, Dépremenil, Géricault, Girault, Larochefoucauld, Renauld, Lecouteulx, Arnoult, Sault, Saulx, Ménilmontant, Ménil-Amelot,** &c., pronounced *arno, chauni, fautier,* &c.

However, l is heard in **Ault, Gréouls,** and **Sainte-Menehould,** pronounced *ôlt, gré-oul, sainte-mene-oul.*

273. l is either silent or liquid, at the option of the speaker, in **Avril, babil, béril, grésil, gentil, fenil, chartil, mil.**

274. And in **avril, péril, babil, béril, bill,** and **mil,** l has also its natural sound.

275. The pronunciation of words which, in the plural, end in **ils,** varies in conformity with their pronunciation in the singular; for instance, **des fusils enlevés** must be pronounced *des fusi-z-enlevés;* and **des outils excellents,** *des*

THEORY AND PRACTICE.

outi-z-excellents; because **fusils** and **outils** do not sound the articulation l in the singular. But **profils exacts, subtils arguments,** must be pronounced *profil-z-exacts, subtil-z-arguments,* because in these words the l is fully sounded in the singular. Likewise, **périls affreux** is pronounced *péri-ȳ-z-affreux,* because the l of **péril** is generally liquid in the singular.

276. In the masculine singular, the l of **gentil** is liquid before a vowel or a mute **h**: everywhere else it is silent. **Un gentil enfant** is pronounced *un genti-ȳ-enfant,* but **de gentils enfants** is pronounced *de genti-z-enfants.* **Gentilhomme** follows this rule: **un gentilhomme,** *un genti-ȳ-homme;* **des gentilshommes,** *des genti-z-hommes.*

277. The only words in which the combination **ill** is not liquid are the following, with all their compounds and derivatives. Those with a star sound the two l's:—

Achille, armillaire.
ă sheel', ăr mee lehr'.

billion, calville.
bee lee ōn, kăl veel'.

Delille, distiller.
duh leel', dees tee la.

Gille, imbécille.
zheel', m̄ ba seel'.

Mabille, *mamillaire.
mă beel', mă meel' lehr'.

*millésime, milliard.
meel la zeehm', mee lee ăr.

million, *osciller.
mee lee ōn, ŏs ceel la.

Priscillien, *pupille.
prees cee lee ĭn, pŭ peell'.

*quintillus, *scille.
kŭ ĭn teel lŭs, seell'.

*stillation, *titiller.
steel lăh see ōn, tee teel la.

myrtille, vaciller.
meer teell', vă seel la

Axillaire, billevesée.
ăk seel lehr', beel' vuh za.

codicille, Cyrille.
kŏ dee seel', see reel'.

fibrille, fritillaire.
fee breel', free tee lehr'.

*instiller, Lille.
ĭns teel la, leel'.

*maxillaire, mille.
măk seel' lehr', meel'.

*milligramme, &c.
meel lee grăm'.

*papillaire, *pénicillé.
pă peel lehr', pa nee seel la.

*pusillanime.
pŭ zeel lă neem'.

scintiller, *sille.
sĭn teel la, seell'.

ville, village, Villèle.
veel', vee lăzh', vee lehl'.

tranquille, squille.
trăn keel', skeel'.

THEORY AND PRACTICE.

278. The following words have now, generally, the liquid sound, which however is not obligatory: **guillemet, guilleret, sillet, fibrille, smille.**

279. The ill of **artillerie** is liquid or not, *ad libitum;* but **artilleur** is always liquid.

280. ill at the beginning of words is never liquid: the two l's are distinctly sounded as in English in *illusion*.

281. When a consonant is doubled, the first is generally silent. This rule applies, to a considerable extent, to the double l; but there are many exceptions. In a number of words, most of which are given on the page opposite, the two l's are distinctly sounded as in English in *collection*. This is always the case in words similar in French and in English, when the two l's are sounded in the latter language.

282. Both l's are distinctly heard in **collation, collationner,** meaning *collation* of writings, *to collate;* but in **collation,** used in the sense of meal, lunch, only one l is pronounced.

283. The combination **ai** before **ll** has the broad sound of **a** in *father*, but in the following words **ai** is pronounced as **a** in *as:* **caillot, caillou, ailleurs, d'ailleurs, Maillard, médaille, vaillance, bataillon,** also in all the tenses of the verbs **détailler, travailler, ravitailler,** and in the tenses of **falloir, valoir,** as well as in those of such verbs of the second conjugation as contain the combination **aill,** and, necessarily, in their derivatives.

PRACTICE.

THIRTY-EIGHTH EXERCISE. *Trente-huitième exercice.*

        [erate.
Illégale, illétré, unlawful, illit-
ĕel la ḡăl', eel la tra.

allégorie, Allah, allegory, Allah.
ăl la ḡo ree, ăl lah.

allusion, allègre, allusion, brisk.
ăl lŭ zee ōn̄, ăl lehgr'.

belligérant, belligerent.
behl lee zha rān̄.

        [allow.
velléités, allouer, velleities, to
vehl la ee ta, ăl loo a.

collationner, to collate.
kŏl lah see ŏ na.

oscillation, oscillation.
ŏs seel lah see ōn̄.

collusion, collusion.
kŏl lŭ zee ōn̄.

constellation, constellation.
kōn̄s tehl lah see ōn̄.

scintillante, scintillating.
sīn̄ teel lān̄t'.

libelliste, libeller.
lee behl leest'.

illusion, delusion.
eel lŭ zee ōn̄.

allocation, allowance.
ăl lŏ kah see ōn̄.

        [amaryllis.
Alluvion, amaryllis, alluvion,
ăl lŭ vee ōn̄, ă mă reel lees.

collocation, collocation.
kŏl lŏ kah see ōn̄.

collatéral, collateral.
kŏl lă ta răl.

intelligence, intelligence.
īn̄ tehl lee zhans'.

pusillanimité, pusillanimity.
pŭ zeel lă nee mee ta.

appellatif, appellative.
ă pehl lă teef.

        [ellipsis.
belladone, ellipse, belladonna,
behl lă dŏn', ehl leeps'.

chambellan, chamberlain.
shān̄ behl lān̄.

circonvallation, circumvallation.
seer kōn̄ văl lah see ōn̄.

        [bore.
syllabe, ellébore, syllable, helle-
seel lăb', ehl la bŏr'.

épellation, villa, spelling, villa.
a pehl lah see ōn̄, veel lă.

villégiature, villeggiatura.
veel la zhee ă tŭr'.

solliciteur, solicitor.
sŏl lee see tuhr.

ă, as; ah, āh, father; uh, ermine; ĕ or ', move; a, late; eh, met; ēh, there; ee, police; ŏ, nor; o, also; ō, no; ŭ, constitution; ēū, first; oo, too; ān̄, want; īn̄, Yankee; ōn̄, don't; ūn̄, grunt; weh, wear; wah, water; ḡ, go; zh, glazier; ḡn̄, singing; ȳ, yes.

THEORY.

THIRTY-NINTH LESSON. *Trente-neuvième leçon.*

CONSONANT L (*continued*).

284. u before il and ill is generally an orthographic letter, and therefore silent: but in **aiguille, cuiller**, and in all their derivatives, also in **Juillet**, the u is fully sounded; forming with the i a diphthong, which is pronounced *ŭ-ee*, — the i announcing, besides, that the following l is liquid.

285. l is liquid (by exception) in the following words: **Choiseul, Broglie, semoule, linceul, Santeul**. (**Sully** is now regularly pronounced.)

286. lh, in the body and at the end of words, is always liquid; and so is the combination ll at the beginning of a few foreign words.

287. Finally and to resume, ll is always liquid when it is preceded by **ai, eai, ei, eui, iai, iei, oai, œi, ouai, oui, uai, uei, uoai**; and l final is liquid also in all the combinations, — **ail, eil, euil, ieil, œil, ouail, ouil, uail, ueil**.

CONSONANT M.

288. m, after a vowel, *in the same syllable*, forms a nasal sound with that vowel.

289. m final forms a nasal sound with the preceding vowel in all French words, whatever their etymology may be.

290. But in words borrowed from foreign languages, m final retains its natural sound (as in *Tom*), except in **Adam, quidam, Absalom, Samson**, and generally **Joachim**, which a long use has Gallicized, and in which m forms a nasal sound.

291. m before n retains its natural sound, and **mn** are pronounced as in English in *amnesty*. However, m is silent in **automne** and **condamner**, and derivatives.

292. The two m's of **imm** at the beginning of words are distinctly pronounced, as in English in *immortal*.

PRACTICE.

THIRTY-NINTH EXERCISE. *Trente-neuvième exercice.*

Le duc de Choiseul, the Duke [of Choiseul.
l' dŭk duh shweh zuhy̆.

le duc de Sully, the Duke of [Sully.
l' dŭk duh sŭl lee.

M. de Broglie, Mr. de Broglie.
muh see eū d' brweh y̆ee.

Milhaut, Milhaut.
mee y̆o.

Pardalhac, Pardalhac.
păr dă y̆ăk.

un linceul, a shroud.
ūn lĭn suhy̆'.

M. de Santeul, Mr. de Santeul.
muh see eū d' sāṉ tuhy̆.

Cruveilhier, Cruveilhier.
krŭ veh y̆ee a.

de la semoule, some semoule.
d' lă s' mooy̆'.

le Lloyd français, the French [Lloyd's.
luh y̆ wehd frāṉ seh.

le Llobregat, the Llobregat.
luh y̆ŏ bruh gă.

Llano Grandé, Llano Grande.
y̆ă no grāṉ da.

Abraham, Abraham.
ă bră ăm.

Stockholm, Stockholm.
stŏ kŏlm.

un item, an item.
ūn nee tehm.

Absalom, Samson, Absalom, [Samson.
ăb să lōṉ, sāṉ sōṉ.

Joachim, Joachim.
zhŏ ă shĭṉ.

l'automne, autumn.
lo tŏn'.

condamnation, condemnation.
kōṉ dah nah see ōṉ.

M. de Condom, Mr. de Condom.
muh see eū d' kōṉ dōṉ.

Riom, le nom, Riom, the name.
ree ōṉ, l' nōṉ.

un essaim, a swarm.
ūn na sĭṉ.

l'immensité, the immensity.
leem māṉ see ta.

indemniser, to indemnify.
ĭṉ dăm nee za.

ă, as; ah, ăh, father; uh, ermine; ĕ or ', move; a, late; eh, met; ēh, there; ee, police; ŏ, nor; o, also; ō, no; ŭ, constitution; eū, first; oo, too; āṉ, want; ĭṉ, Yankee; ōṉ, don't; ūṉ, grunt; weh, wear; wah, water; ḡ, go; zh, glazier; ḡū, singing; y̆, yes.

THEORY.

FORTIETH LESSON. *Quarantième leçon.*

CONSONANT M (*continued*).

293. **em** prefixed to words and having the character of a preposition retains the nasal pronunciation, even before another **m**. The only exceptions are **Emma, Emmanuel, Emmaüs, emménagogue, emménalogie, emmésostome,** in which the two **m**'s retain their proper sound.

294. In **emm**, in the middle of words, the first **m** is silent, the second has the proper sound (as in *me*), and the **e** is sounded as **a** in *as*.

295. But **lemme, dilemme, gemme,** and **gemmation** sound the two **m**'s.

296. Both m's are also sounded in **grammatiste, grammatical, Ammon, nummulaire,** and a few others of foreign origin.

OBS.—Substantives ending in **m** or **n** nasal never carry the final **m** or **n** to the next word.

297. All words ending in **um** are borrowed from the Latin (except **parfum,** which is derived, not borrowed, from it); and the termination **um** is always pronounced *ome*,—o as in *none*.

298. **rumb** or **rhumb** and **parfum** are pronounced *ronb, parfun*.

CONSONANT N.

299. **n** followed by a vowel or a mute **h**, in the body of a word, begins the syllable, and is pronounced as in English in *nine;* but in **enarbrer, enivrer, enorgueillir,** and in all their derivatives, the particle **en**, which has the character of a preposition, retains the nasal sound, and the **n**, regularly carried to **arbrer, ivrer,** and **orgueillir,** assumes naturally the proper sound.

300. **n** before a consonant, except **n** and **h** mute, forms a nasal sound with the preceding vowel.

PRACTICE.

FORTIETH EXERCISE. *Quarantième exercice.*

Les omnibus, la zŏm nee büs.	the omnibuses.	**Nemrod,** nehm rŏd.	Nimrod.
la calomnie, lă kă lŏm nee.	the calumny.	**le Kremlin,** l' krehm liñ.	the Kremlin.
diligemment, dee lee zhă mañ.	diligently.	**triumvir,** tree ŏm veer.	triumvir.
Emmanuel, ehm mă nü ehl.	Emmanuel.	**décemvir,** da sehm veer.	decemvir.
omnipotence, ŏm nee pŏ tañs'.	omnipotence.	**elle s'enorgueillit,** ehl' sañ nŏr g̃uh ẏee.	[herself proud. she makes
emmêler, añ meh la.	to entangle.	**l'enivrement,** lañ nee vruh mañ.	the intoxication.
une lampe, ün' lañp'.	a lamp.	**inhabile,** ee nă beel'.	unskilful.
un dilemme, üñ dee lehmm'.	a dilemma.	**enivrante,** añ nee vrañt'.	intoxicating.
grammaticalement, g̃răm mă tee kăl' mañ.	grammati-[cally.	**sciemment,** see ă mañ.	knowingly.
un pensum, üñ piñ sŏm.	a school task.	**du rhum,** dü rŏm.	some rum.
l'iridium, lee ree dee ŏm.	iridium.	**le macadam,** l' mă kă dăm.	the macadam.
un post-scriptum, üñ pŏst skreep tŏm.	a postscript.	**la timballe,** lă tiñ băl'.	the timbal.

ă, as; ah, äh, father; uh, ermine; ĕ or ', move; a, late; eh, met; ēh, there; ee, police; ŏ, nor; o, also; ō, no; ŭ, constitution; ēü, first; oo, too; añ, want; iñ, Yankee; oñ, don't; üñ, grunt; weh, **w**ear; wah, **w**ater; g̃, go; zh, glazier; g̃ñ, sing-ing; ẏ, yes.

FRENCH PRONUNCIATION.

THEORY.

FORTY-FIRST LESSON. *Quarante et unième leçon.*

CONSONANT *N* (*continued*).

301. In the case of double **n**, the first is generally silent, and does not form a nasal sound with the preceding vowel, which, of course, retains its proper sound. (For the exceptions, see below.)

302. But in **ennui, ennoblir, ennasser,** and in all their derivatives, the syllable **en** has the character of a preposition. As such, it retains the nasal sound; and the second **n**, beginning the syllable, has its natural sound.

303. **en** is pronounced **a**, as in *as*, in the following words and in their derivatives: **hennir, nenni, rouennais, solennel,** and **s'ennuiter.**

304. **en** is pronounced as **an** in *Yankee.*

1°. At the beginning and in the middle of words of foreign origin.

2°. In the body of almost all foreign, and a few French, proper names.

3°. In the persons of the verbs terminated in the infinitive in **venir** and **tenir**, whenever **ien** is not followed by **n**.

4°. At the end of French substantives and proper names, and foreign proper names terminated in **ien** and **éen**.

305. When the particle **in** of **inn**, at the beginning of words, has the force of a negation, the two **n**'s are distinctly sounded, without nasality. Both **n**'s are also sounded in a few words, a list of which is given on the page opposite.

306. The particle **in**, prefixed to words borrowed from the Latin, is pronounced *een;* but in the library terms **in-folio, in-quarto, in-douze, in-seize,** &c., which a frequent use has Gallicized, **in** retains the nasal sound. **In-plano** and **in-octavo** have retained, however, the Latin pronunciation.

307. **n** final forms a nasal sound with the preceding vowel; but in proper names and in a number of words of foreign origin ending in **n** or **nn**, the **n**'s retain the natural sound (as in *man, hen*).

308. **n** final in substantives, if otherwise silent, is never carried to the next word.

PRACTICE.

FORTY-FIRST EXERCISE. *Quarante et unième exercice.*

Il hennissait,   it neighed.
eel å nee seh.
                    [mennais.
M. de Lamennais, Mr. de La-
muh see eū d' lăm neh.
cela ennoblit,   that does exalt.
s' lă an nŏ blee.
                [out late at night.
vous vous ennuitez, you stay
voo voo ză nŭ ee ta.
une solennité,   a solemnity.
ŭn' sŏ lă nee ta.
un rouennais, a native of Rouen.
ŭn̄ roo ă neh.
Benjamin,   Benjamin.
bin̄ zhă min̄.
Mentor, inné, Mentor, innate.
min̄ tŏr, een na.
                [school task.
Rubens, pensum, Rubens,
rŭ bin̄s, pin̄ sŏm.
le Camoëns,   le Camoens.
luh kă-mŏ in̄s.
                    [tor.
Ecouen, stentor, Ecouen, sten-
a koo in̄, stin̄ tŏr.
Saint-Ouen,   Saint Ouen.
sin̄ too in̄.

L'examen,   the examination.
lag ză min̄.
un spencer,   a spencer.
ŭn̄ spin̄ sehr.
du benjoin,   some benzoin.
dŭ bin̄ zhŏ in̄.
un agenda, a memorandum book.
ŭn̄ năzhin̄dă.
                  [entered.
il vient d'entrer, he has just
eel vee in̄ dān̄ tra.
les européens,   Europeans.
la zeū rŏ pa in̄.
un in-octavo,   an octavo.
ŭn̄ nee nŏk tă vo.
un in-douze,   a duodecimo.
ŭn̄ nin̄ dooz'.
                [the spleen.
l'in-folio, le spleen, the folio,
lin̄ fŏ lee o, luh spleen.
innombrable,   innumerable.
een nŏn̄ brăbl'.
le Béarn, Eden, Béarn, Eden.
l' ba ărn', a dehn.
                  [behen.
le lichen, béhen, the lichen,
luh lee kehn, ba ehn.

ă, as; ah, âh, father; uh, ermine; ĕ or ', move; a, late; eh, met; ēh, there; ee, police; ŏ, nor; o, also; ō, no; ŭ, constitution; eū, first; oo, too; ān̄, want; in̄, Yankee; ōn̄, don't; ŭn̄, grunt; weh, wear; wah, water; ḡ, go; zh, glazier; ḡn̄, singing; ȳ, yes.

THEORY.

FORTY-SECOND LESSON. *Quarante-deuxième leçon.*

CONSONANT *N (continued).*

309. In poetry, when rhyme demands it, **Eden** is pronounced *édèn*.

310. **Le Béarn**, a French province, sounds the **n**; but in **M. de Béarn** the **n** is silent (in good society). **Talleyrand, Lamennais, Sennecterre,** are pronounced *talran, lamnè, sèn' terre.*

311. The **n** of **en**, preposition, is always carried to the next word, when the latter begins with a vowel.

bien, adverb, **rien** and **un,** pronouns, are joined to the following word when they are connected to it in sense, or when euphony requires it.

The **n** of **mon, ton, son,** is always carried to the next word.

un carries its **n** to the following word, but only when the latter is a noun or an adjective with which **un** is intimately connected in sense.

en and **on,** pronouns, are joined only to verbs to which they belong.

The **n** of **ent**, termination of the third person plural of verbs, is always silent.

Adjectives ending in **n,** as **bon, vilain, ancien, plein, certain,** &c., carry the **n** to the next word, but only when that word is a noun to which they are inseparably united; that is, when the sense does not admit the slightest pause between them. The nasality of the last syllable of the adjective may disappear, and the vowel preceding the final **n** reassume its natural sound; *but this is optional.* The ease or the difficulty of pronunciation is a sufficient guide in this case.

CONSONANT P.

312. **p** initial is always sounded in French.

313. **p** final is pronounced in **Alep, bishop, calp, cap, croup, escap, escoup, Gap, group, hanap, hap! houp! jalap, julep, kanaap, piahiap, salep, sep, sloop, tap, trapp, tsia-ip,** and **tsiap.**

THEORY AND PRACTICE.

CONSONANT P (*continued*).

314. The p of **trop** and **beaucoup** is carried to the next word, beginning with a vowel, when no pause can be made between the two words: —

Il est trop entêté pour céder, eel eh trŏ pāū teh ta poor sa da.	He is too headstrong to yield.
J'ai beaucoup étudié, zha bo koo pa tü dee a.	I have studied very much.

Everywhere else **p** final is silent, *even before a vowel*.

315. p not final is fully sounded, except in the following words and in their compounds and derivatives: **baptême, baptiser, Baptiste, cheptel, compter, corps, exempt, printemps, prompt, sculpter, temps, Troplong, dompter, je romps, tu romps, il rompt, Wimpffen.**

316. The p of **champ** at the beginning of nouns is silent before consonants, except before l: **Champcenetz, Champfleury, Champmeslé**, &c., pronounced *chansnè, chanfleuri, chanmélé*, &c. But the p is heard in **Champlain, Champlatreux**, &c. At the end of nouns, the p of **champ** and **camp** is never pronounced: **Decamps, Longchamps**, &c., are pronounced *decan, lonchan*, &c.

317. The p of **sept, septième, septièmement**, is also silent; but it is heard in all the other words beginning with **sept**.

318. When p is doubled, the second only is sounded, except in a few Greek proper names; such as **Agrippa, Hippomène, Hippias, Agrippine**, &c. **Appétence** and **appéter** sound also the two p's.

319. In **trop**, *too much*, the o is sounded as in **nor**, when **trop** precedes the word it modifies; but when **trop** follows that word, its o is sounded as in *also*.

J'ai trop d'ouvrage, zha trŏ doo vrăzh'.	I have too much work.
J'en ai trop, zhāṅ na tro.	I have too much of it.

THEORY.

CONSONANT Q.

320. q is always followed by u; except in coq, cinq, Boscq, Ouroq, Dubocq, Saint-Criocq, Vicq-D'Azyr, and a few other proper names, where it is final, and sounded as k in *key*.

321. q is always sounded in coq. (The vulgar pronunciation of coq d'Inde — *co-d'Inde* — is inadmissible among educated people.)

322. The q of cinq is fully sounded, except when cinq is immediately followed by a substantive, a qualifying adjective, or a number, beginning with a consonant, and provided cinq be connected in sense with those words.

323. Cinq-Mars is pronounced *sin-mar;* and quanquam, aquosité, and piqûre, are respectively pronounced *kwan-kwam, a ku o sité,* and *pi kur'*.

CONSONANT R.

324. At the beginning and in the body of a word r is fully sounded, except in gars, Angers, and in all the words ending in iers. However, r is heard in le Chiers, Thiers, un tiers, and in the termination iers of the verbs ending in the infinitive in quérir.

325. r final is sounded in all the terminations that are not er; but r is silent in monsieur, messieurs, and oublieur.

326. er final is pronounced as the English word ere.

1°. In foreign proper names.
2°. In monosyllabic words and in their compounds.
3°. In a few French proper names: —

Auber, Abd-el-kader, le Cher, Albert Durer, Fanny Elssler,
o behr, abd ehl kä dehr, luh shehr, äl behr dü rehr, fän nee ehl slehr,

Esther, Gessler, Gessner, Jupiter, Kléber, Necker, Lucifer,
ehs tehr, ğehs lehr, ğehs nehr, zhü pee tehr, kla behr, neh kehr, lü see fehr,

Pont-Audemer, Quimper, Reuter, Rœderer, Rouher, Suger,
pōn to d' mehr, kiñ pehr, röū tehr, ra duh rehr, roo ehr, sü zhehr.

St. Sever, &c.
siñ suh vehr.

4°. In a number of polysyllabic words, the most frequently used of which are given on the page opposite.

PRACTICE.

FORTY-SECOND EXERCISE. *Quarante-deuxième exercice.*

Certain endroit, certain place.
sehr tĭñ nāñ drweh.

le bien et le mal, good and evil.
l' bee m̄ a l' măl.
[vicious.

vilain et vicieux, ugly and
vee lĭñ a vee see ēū.
[not?

est-il bon ou non? is it good or
eh teel bōñ oo nōñ.
in Egypt?

pleut-il en Egypte? does it rain
pleū teel āñ na zheept'.

du reps, some reps.
dŭ rehps.

le relaps, the relapser.
luh r' lăps.

une crypte, a crypt.
ŭn' kreept'.

l'éclipse, the eclipse.
la kleeps'.

un sculpteur, a sculptor.
ŭñ skŭl tuhr.

présomptueux, presumptuous.
pra zōñp tŭ ēū.

pneumatique, pneumatic.
pnēū mă teek'.
[may be.

quoique ce soit, whatever it
kweh kuh suh sweh.

vétiver, bent-grass.
va tee vehr.

Amer, aster, bitter, aster.
ă mehr, ăs tehr.
[day.

auster, hier, south wind, yester-
ŏs tehr, ee ehr.
[bitter.

belvéder, bitter, belvidere,
behl va dehr, bee tehr.
[cancer.

calender, cancer, calendar,
kă lăñ dehr, kāñ sehr.

cher, coroner, dear, coroner.
shehr, kŏ rŏ nehr.

cutter, cuiller, cutter, spoon.
kŭ tehr, kŭ ee yehr.

eider, enfer, eider, hell.
a dehr, āñ fehr.

éther, fer, fier, ether, iron, proud.
a tehr, fehr, fee ehr.
[wehr.

hiver, landwehr, winter, land-
ee vehr, lāñd vehr.

lavander, lavender.
lă vāñ dehr.

mâchefer, slag.
māhsh' fehr.
[ter.

magister, mer, school-master,
mă zhees tehr, mehr.
[ultramarine.

revolver, outremer, revolver,
ruh vŏl vehr, oo truh mehr.

thaler, ver, thaler, worm.
tah lehr, vehr.

ă, as; ah, âh, father; uh, ermine; ĕ or ', move; a, late; eh, met; ēh, there; ee, police; ŏ, nor; o, also; ō, no; ŭ, constitution; ēū, first; oo, too; āñ, want; īñ, Yankee; ōñ, don't; ūñ, grunt; weh, wear; wah, water; ḡ, go; zh, glazier; ḡn, singing; ȳ, yes.

THEORY AND PRACTICE.

FORTY-THIRD LESSON. *Quarante-troisième leçon.*

CONSONANT R (*continued*).

327. **r** final is mute, and the **e** preceding it is sounded as **a** in *late*.

1°. In **Alger** and **Tanger**.
2°. In French proper names, except those mentioned in § 326.
3°. At the end of all substantives terminating in **er**, except those given on p. 109.
4°. At the end of adjectives in **er**.
5°. At the end of all words in **ier** and **yer**. Five words only form an exception to this last rule: **hier, fier** (adj.), **avant-hier, laemmer-geier, myer**.
6°. At the end of all verbs of the first conjugation. However, in poetry, in the noble style, and generally in serious reading, the **r** of the infinitive is carried to the next word when the latter begins with a vowel.

328. The **r** of adjectives ending in **ier** is carried to the next word, but only when that word is a substantive modified by the adjective: —

Vous écrirez le premier exercice, You will write the first exercise.
voo za kree ra l' pruh mee a ra ḡzehr sees'.

329. **r**, before **d, s,** and **t** final, is fully sounded; the **d, s,** and **t** being generally silent, even before a vowel. But **fort**, adv., **sert**, verb, and **vers**, prep., usually carry their final consonant to the next word: —

Vous aurez fort à faire, You will have much to do.
voo zŏ ra fŏr tă fehr.
Cela ne sert à rien, That is of no use.
s' lă n' sehr tă ree m̄.

THEORY AND PRACTICE.

CONSONANT R (continued).

330. Both r's are sounded, —

1°. In the forty-three following words: **aberration, Burrhus, concurremment, corroborant, corroboratif, corroboration, corroborer, corrodant, corroder, corrosif, corrosion, errant, errata, erratique, erratum, errer, erreur, errhin, erroné, farrago, horreur, horrible, horriblement, horripilation, inérarrable, intercurrent, interrègne, myrrhis, narration, porrection, Pyrrha, pyrrhique, pyrrhonisme, Pyrrhus, sarrasalme, torréfaction, torréfier, torride, terreur, terrible, terriblement, Urraque, Verrès.**

2°. In all words beginning with **irr.**

3°. In the future and conditional of the verb **mourir,** and of all the verbs in **courir** and **quérir.**

4°. In Perrault's sentence: **la bobinette cherra.**

Everywhere else, when r is doubled, the first is silent.

331. **rh** is always pronounced as **r** alone.

CONSONANT S.

332. **s** at the beginning of words is sounded as in **so**, even before a consonant; but when **s**, initial or not, is immediately followed by a soft consonant, as **b, d, g, j, v,** it naturally takes the soft sound *zuh*, which easily coalesces with those consonants; hence **sb, sd, sg, sj, sv,** must be pronounced *zb, zd, zg, zj, zv.*

333. In the middle of words, and preceded or followed by a consonant, **s** is sounded as in *so*. It is silent in **est, is.**

334. **s** preceding **ce** or **ci** in the body of a word is felt rather than fully pronounced. The voice glides slightly over the **s**, but distinctly articulates the **c**.

335. **s** is regularly pronounced as in **so** in the terminations **asme, isme.** The pronunciation *azme, izme,* is a provincialism to be carefully guarded against.

FRENCH PRONUNCIATION.

THEORY AND PRACTICE.

CONSONANT S (*continued*).

336. When, in compound words, **s** is the initial letter of the simple; as in **vraisemblable**, compounded of *vrai* and *semblable ;* **présupposer, parasol, monosyllabe,** &c., it retains its regular sound (as in *so*).

337. It has also the same sound (as in so) in : **gisant,** *lying,* **gisons, gisais, gisiez, gisaient, gisez, gisent, gisait, gisions.**

338. **s** is fully sounded as in so in the termination **us** of words borrowed from the Latin : **blocus, prospectus, omnibus,** &c.

339. **s** final is also sounded in a large number of words and proper names, the greater proportion of which have been taken from the Latin and Greek languages; the most frequently used are given here : **albatros, albinos, aloès, amaryllis, ambesas, as, atlas, bis, cassis, cens, contre-sens, cortès, creps, diabétès, éléphantiasis, ès, express, extramuros, fils, florès, gneiss, gratis, hélas, hypocras, ibis, iris, jadis, lapis-lazuli, laps, lis, locatis, madras, maïs, makis, mars, méfitis, mérinos, métis, mœurs, non-sens, oasis, os, ours, pathos, plus, plus-que-parfait, rachitis, relaps, reps, rhinocéros, sens, strass, tétanos, tournevis, tous, unguis, vasistas, vindas, vis, volubilis.**

340. **s** final is also sounded in foreign proper names and in a few French names : **Agnès, Anglès, Arlès-Dufour, Arras, Assas, Athénaïs, Atlas, Aunis, Baradas, Barras, Baumès, Blacas, Boissy d'Anglas, Brancas, Brennus, Brueys, Cabanis, Calas, Calvados, Cambacérès, Carpentras, Caylus, Cazalès, Charondas, Clovis, Cujus, Damas, Drouin de Lhuys, Ducis, Duras, Esquiros, Exelmans, Flourens, Garnier-Pagès, Genlis, Havas, Las-Cases, Lesseps, Mazas, Mirès, Paixhans, Rheims, Senlis, Sens, Uzès, Vaugelas, Vestris, Warens,** &c.

PRACTICE.

FORTY-THIRD EXERCISE.   *Quarante-troisième exercice.*

J'acquérais,	I acquired.	J'acquerrais,	I would acquire.
zhă kạ reh.		zhă kehr reh.	
il courait,	he was running.	il courrait,	he would run.
eel koo reh.		eel koor reh.	
je suis enrhumé,	I have a cold.		[mange.
zhuh süee zăn rü mạ.		du blanc-manger,	some blanc-
	[will fall.	dü blăn măn zha.	
la bobinette cherra,	the bobbin	Sganarelle,	Sganarelle.
lă bŏ bee neht' shehr ră.		zg̅ă nă rehl'.	
	[joined.	une disgrâce,	a disgrace.
le sbire, disjoint,	the sbirro, dis-	ün' deez g̅răhs'.	
luh zbeer', deez zhŏ ĭn.		substance,	substance.
l'enthousiasme,	the enthusiasm.	süb stăns'.	
lăn too zee ăsm'.		sciemment,	knowingly.
spongieux,	spongy.	see ă măn.	
spŏn zhee eū.		Asnières,	Asnières.
l'Aisne,	the Aisne.	ah nee ehr'.	
lehn'.		Chastellux,	Chastellux.
Desmoulins,	Desmoulins.	shăh t' lü.	
dạ moo lĭn.		L'Espinasse,	L'Espinasse.
Laubespine,	Laubespine.	la pee năs'.	
lo bạ peen'.		Saint-Priest,	Saint-Priest.
Praslin,	Praslin.	sĭn pree.	
prah lĭn.		Du Guesclin,	Du Guesclin.
Vosgien,	Vosgien.	dü g̅ạ klĭn.	
vo zhee ĭn.			[Chasles.
Rosny,	Rosny.	Philarète Chasles,	Philarète
ro nee.		fee lă rēht' shăhl'.	

ă, as ; ah, ăh, father ; uh, ermine ; ĕ or ', move ; a, late ; eh, met ; ēh, there ; ee, police ; ŏ, nor ; o, also ; ō, no ; ŭ, constitution ; eū, first ; oo, too ; ăn, want ; ĭn, Yankee ; ŏn, don't ; ŭn, grunt ; weh, **wear** ; wah, **water** ; g̅, go ; zh, glazier ; g̅n, singing ; y̅, yes.

THEORY AND PRACTICE.

FORTY-FOURTH LESSON. *Quarante-quatrième leçon.*

CONSONANT S (*continued*).

341. **Bis**, *encore*, sounds the **s**; but **s** is silent in **bis**, *brown*.

342. **Sens**, *sense*, sounds its final **s**, except in the five expressions: —

Sens commun, common sense.
sān kŏ mūn.

sens dessus dessous, topsy-
sān d' sŭ d' soo.
[turvy.
[before.

sens devant derrière, hind part
sān d' vān deh ree ehr'.

Bon sens, good sense.
bōn sān.

de sens rassis, unmoved.
d' sān ră see.

343. The **s** of **plus**, adv. forming a comparative or superlative, and of **plus** negative, is silent before a consonant: it is sounded as **z** before a vowel. But the **s** of **plus**, *more*, positive, is generally slightly pronounced, as **s** in *so* before a consonant, but only when a short pause can be made after **plus**; before a vowel **s** naturally assumes the sound of **z**: —

La religion est nécessaire: je dis plus, elle est indispensable.
lă r' lee zhee ōn eh na sa sehr': zh' dee plŭs, ehl' eh tīn dees pān sǎbl'.

Je vous ai payé tout, et mille francs en plus.
zh' voo za peh ya too, a meel' frān zān plŭs.

Voici mon billet, plus, la somme de cent francs.
vweh see mōn bee yeh, plŭs, lă sŏm' duh sān frān.

344. **Lis**, *lily*, sounds its **s**, except in **Fleur-de-lis** (heraldic term).

345. The **s** of **fils**, *son*, is sounded; but in circumstances of great solemnity, and in poetry, when the exigencies of the rhyme demand it, the **s** of **fils** may be silent: —

Et de ses doigts glacés prenant le crucifix:
a duh sa dweh glă sa pruh nān luh krŭ see fee.

Voilà le souvenir, et voilà l'espérance!
vweh lă luh soo vuh neer, a vwehlă la spa rāns'.

Emportez-les, mon fils! — LAMARTINE.
ān pŏr ta la, mōn fee.

346. **Tous**, *all*, pronoun, sounds the **s**; **tous**, adjective, does not: —

Tous fuyaient, all were running
toos fŭ ee yeh.
[away.

tous les hommes, all men.
too la zŏm'.

Nous irons tous, we shall all go.
noo zee rōn toos.

venez tous les deux, come,
v' na too la deū.
[both of you.

THEORY AND PRACTICE.

CONSONANT S (continued).

347. We have already seen that **s** final is sounded in foreign proper names, but it is silent when they end in **es**: **Londres, Douvres,** &c., pronounced *londr', douvr'*.

348. **s**, which is sounded in **Christ, le Christ,** is silent in **Jésus-Christ,** and **antechrist.**

349. **Jésus, Thomas, Nicolas,** and **Judas,** although of foreign origin, do not sound their final **s**.

350. In good society, **M. de Brancas** and **M. de Damas** suppress the **s** sound. **De Castries** is pronounced *de castr'*; and **Desaix,** *duh seh.*

351. The combination **es** of the reduplicative particle **res** is sounded as **e** in *ermine*, before **s**; the **es** of **dessus** and **dessous** has also the same sound, but the **e** sound may be slighted or dropped when necessary: —

Ressembler, le ressort, se ressouvenir, dessus, la ressource,
ruh sān bla, luh ruh sŏr, suh ruh soov' neer, duh sŭ, lă ruh soors',

dessous; or, **ressembler, ressort, ressouvenir, dessus, res-**
duh soo. r' sān bla, r' sŏr, r' soov' neer, d' sŭ, r'

source, dessous, ressemelage.
soors', d' soo, r' suh m' lăzh'.

352. But in the four words which follow, the **e** of **es** is regularly sounded as **a** in *late*: —

[dry.	[the surf.
Le ressui, ressuyer, the lair, to	**ressusciter, le ressac,** to revive,
luh ra sŭ ee, ra sŭ ee ya.	ra sŭ see ta, luh ra săk.

353. **s** between two consonants is fully sounded and forms a part of the same syllable with the first: —

[spire, to inscribe.	**Pers-pective,** perspective.
Cons-pirer, inscrire, to con-	pehrs pehk teev'.
kōns pee ra, īns kreer'.	
s'abs-tenir, to abstain.	**obs-curité,** darkness.
săbs tuh neer.	ŏbs kŭ ree ta.

354. **s** followed by a consonant is distinctly sounded; and, when both letters belong to the same syllable, the consonant is sounded with the **s**; otherwise, each letter is sounded with the syllable to which it belongs: —

Stimulants, prestidigitateur, flosculeux, mascarade, stigmate.
stee mŭ lān, prehs tee dee zhee tă tuhr, flŏs kŭ leū, măs kă răd', steeg măt'.

THEORY AND PRACTICE.

CONSONANT S (*continued*).

355. When **s** is double the first is silent. But in poetry and in the elevated style both **s**'s are sounded in: **assa fœtida, asservir, asservissement, amplissime, bellissime, compressible, généralissime, grandissime, illustrissime, intussusception, Manassès, Nessus, rarissime, richissime, transsudation, transsubstantiation, vicissitude, assentiment, assonance, dissonance, missive, fissure, inadmissible, scission,** &c.

356. **s** before **ce, ci,** and **cy,** is silent: **plébiscite, fascine, escient, s'immiscer, prescience,** &c. However, the **s** is sounded in **ascyre, ascétique, concupiscible, fascicule, irascible, proscénium, rarescible, rarescibilité.**

357. Followed by **en,** both the letters **sc** are pronounced with the hissing sound of **s** in *so*: **ascension, condescendre, effervescent, transcendant,** &c. But in the following five words the **s** is silent: *descendance, descendant, descendre, descente, redescendre.*

358. **s** is sounded as **z** in *zone* (soft sound), —
1°. Between two vowels.
2°. Before **b, d, g,** and **j.**
3°. In the Latin syllable **trans** followed by a vowel, except in *transir, transept, Transylvanie,* and their derivatives.
4°. In the following words and those of the same radical:—

Alsace, Arsace, asthme, balsamine, subsister, Israël, Ismaël,
ăl zăs', ăr zăs', ăzm', băl ză meen', sŭb zees ta, eez ră ehl, eez mă ehl,
bismuth, Belsunce, Bethsabée, Nansouty, transvaser.
beez mŭt, behl zŭñs', beht ză ba, naū zoo tee, trāūz vah za.

5°. Before **b** and **d,** because of the natural attraction.

Asbestre, bisbille, Dresde, presbytère, transborder, Esdras, &c.
ăz behstr', beez beeyĕ, drehzd', prehz bee tehr', trāūz bŏr da, ehz drahs.

359. **s** added to form the plural does not change the pronunciation of the syllable, it lengthens its sound. In conversation, however, this alteration is hardly perceptible.

THEORY AND PRACTICE.

CONSONANT S (concluded).

360. s final carried to the next word assumes the z sound.

361. It is an elegance of elocution, when using in the plural those words which sound their final s in the singular, not only to carry the s sounded as z to the next word, but to let the hissing sound of s (as in *so*) be heard slightly before the connection takes place; both the hissing and the hard sound being produced in quick succession. The requisite delicacy of the movements of the organs in these circumstances always and with unerring certainty indicates education, good breeding, and refinement: —

Les mœurs anglaises,   Les fils et les pères,   Les mérinos
la ˚muhrs zañ ḡlehz'.   la fees za la pĕhr',   la ma ree nŏs
espagnols.
zas pă ḡnŏl.

362. The final s is never carried to the following words, — oui, onze, ouate, and un, une, numeral adjectives.

OBS. — The familiar expression **entre quatre yeux** is, by reason of euphony, pronounced *entre quatre-z-yeux*. (See Dict. of the Acad.) Moreover, **quatre** was formerly spelled *quatres*: it is not surprising that the s sound (as z) should have been retained. Some authors write **entre quatre-z-yeux**, the anomaly, if there is any, thus disappearing.

CONSONANT T.

363. In a few foreign proper names, t feeling the influence of the following z is pronounced d: **Dantzick, Fitz-Gérald,** &c.

364. t retains its proper sound (as in *tax*), —
1°. At the beginning of words.
2°. In the middle of words when it is not followed by i and another vowel.
3°. Before y, except in **amphictyons** and der., pron. *anfiksion*.
4°. In **the**, whatever place th occupies in the word.

365. When **haut** enters into the composition of a word, its t is silent before a consonant, sounded before a vowel.

THEORY AND PRACTICE.

CONSONANT T (continued).

366. The **t** of **mont** and **pont**, at the beginning of words, is also silent before consonants, sounded before vowels.

However, t is sounded by exception in **Montredon, Montrejean, Montrésor, Montret, Montretout, Montreuil, Montrevault, Montrevel, Montrichard, Pontremoli,** and **Pontrieux.**

COMBINATION TI.

367. The **t** of **ti** is pronounced as in *tax*,—

1°. After **s** or **x**.

2°. In the syllables **tié, tiers, tier, tiè,** and **thie,** except **initier, satiété,** and in the five verbs **argutier, balbutier, différentier, initier,** and **transsubstantier,** words in which **tié** and **tier** are pronounced *sié*.

3°. In the syllable **tie** preceded by a consonant; with the exception of **gilbertie, ineptie, inertie, rhinoptie,** pronounced *gilbersie, inepsie,* &c.

4°. In the feminine terminations **tie** and **ties** of past participles, and in all the parts of the verb **châtier.**

5°. In **tième** and **tièmement.**

6°. In the syllables **tien** and **tienne.** But in proper names (except **Chrétien**), the t of **tien, tienne,** takes the sound of **s.** (See p. 120, 8°.)

7°. In **centiare, éléphantiasis, Critias, étiage, galimatias, tiare,** and in words containing **antia,** as **antiacide,** &c. Everywhere else **tia** is pronounced *sia*.

8°. In **étioler** and deriv. in **commation, Bagration,** and **Pétion,** everywhere else **tio** and **tion** are pronounced **sio, sion.**

9°. In the terminations **tions, tiez,** of the first and second persons plural of verbs, except in those given above. (See 2°.)

10°. Finally in **rôtie, sotie, tutie, Clytie, Orithye, épizootie, philautie.**

CONSONANTS.   119

PRACTICE.

FORTY-FOURTH EXERCISE. *Quarante-quatrième exercice.*

Fitz-James, Fitz-James.
feedz zhăm'.
                                    [height.
le tiers, hauteur, the third part,
l' tee ehr,   o tuhr.
                                    [tented.
tu es contente, thou art con-
tü eh kōn tānt'.
un bastion, a bastion.
ŭn băs tee ōn.
la gestion, the management.
lă zhehs tee ōn.
les mixtions, the mixtures.
la meeks tee ōn.
tu châtieras, thou wilt chastise.
tü shăh tee ră.
la sympathie, the sympathy.
lă sīn pă tee.
la pitié, pity.
lă pee tee a.
                                    [mathy.
la chrestomathie, the chresto-
lă krehs tŏ mă tee.
arbres fruitiers, fruit-trees.
ărbr' frü ee tee a.
une ortie, a nettle.
ün' ŏr tee.
la dynastie, the dynasty.
lă dee năs tee.

Elle est aplatie, it is flattened.
ehl' eh tă plă tee.
                                  [them.
je les ai averties, I warned
zh' la za ă vehr tee.
nous portions, we carried.
noo pŏr tee ōn.
le maintien, the maintenance.
l' mīn tee īn.
ils obtiennent, they obtain.
eel zŏb tee ehn'.
la Tchernaïa, the Tchernaia.
lă tshehr nă ee ă,
Tlemsen, Tlemsen.
tlehm sehn.
Bitche, Bastia, Bitche, Bastia.
beetsh', băs tee ă.
Hautpoul, Hautpoul.
o pool.
Montréal, Montreal.
mōn ra ăl.
Montpensier, Montpensier.
mōn pān see a.
Montlhéry, Montlhéry.
mōn la ree.
Pontchartrain, Pontchartrain.
pōn shăr trīn.

ă, as; ah, äh, father; uh, ermine; ĕ or ', move; a, late; eh, met; ēh, there; ee, police; ŏ, nor; o, also; ō, no; ŭ, constitution; eū, first; oo, too; ān, want; īn, Yankee; ōn, don't; ūn, grunt; weh, wear; wah, water; g̃, go; zh, glazier; g̃n, singing; ȳ, yes.

THEORY AND PRACTICE.

FORTY-FIFTH LESSON. *Quarante-cinquième leçon.*

COMBINATION *TI* (*continued*).

368. The combination ti is pronounced **see**.

1°. In **patient** and all its derivatives; in **partient**, component part of some mathematical terms, and in **quotient**.
2°. In the syllable **tia**. (See exceptions, six words, page 118, 7°.)
3°. In the syllables **tiaux, tiel, tieux, tieuse**, and **tius**, without exception.
4°. In the termination **tiaire**, without exception.
5°. In the syllable **tio**, one exception. (See p. 118, 8°.)
6°. In **tion**. (See the three exceptions, p. 118, 8°.)
7°. In the termination **tium**.
8°. In the syllable **tien**, when it terminates names of persons, peoples, sects, &c. (See p. 118, 6°.)
9°. In the terminations **atie, étie, itie, otie, utie**, five exceptions. (See p. 118, 10°.)
10°. Finally the **ti** is pronounced **see** in **gilbertie, ineptie, inertie, rhinoptie**; in all the parts of the five verbs **argutier, balbutier, différentier, initier, transsubstantier,** and in **initié, satiété,** and **balbutiement**.

T FINAL.

369. t final is generally silent; it is, however, sounded before consonants as before vowels in all the following words: abject, abrupt, accessit, aconit, apt, arrowroot, azimut, balast, brut, Christ, chut! cobalt, compact, compost, comput, contact, correct, déficit, direct, dot, échec et mat, l'est, exact, exeat, fat, flat, granit, hast, heurt, huit, incorrect, indirect, indult, inexact, inhalt, infect, intact, intellect, knout, lest, licet, lut, malt, mat, obit, occiput, opiat, ouest, pat, prétérit, quant à, quartz, rapt, rit, raout, rut, sedlitz, sinciput, smalt, spalt, spint, steamboat, strict, tact, tacet, toast, transept, transit, tut, uranit, ut, véniat, vivat, whist, le zist et le zest.

NOTE. — We have omitted only a few words, seldom used.

THEORY AND PRACTICE.

CONSONANT T (*continued*).

370. The final t is generally sounded in the following words: however, it is not incorrect not to pronounce it:—

Distinct, fret, indistinct, net, succinct, suspect, test, vermout.
dees tĭn̄kt, freht, ĭn̄ dees tĭn̄ct, neht, sŭk sĭn̄t, sŭs pehkt, tehst, vehr moot.

371. Per contra, t is generally silent in the six words below; but it is optional to pronounce it or not:—

Alphabet, aspect, circonspect, fait, respect, sot.
ăl fă beh, ăs pehk, seer kōn̄s pehk, feh, res pehk, so.

372. **Sept** and **huit** sound the t, except before a substantive or an adjective beginning with a consonant, and which **sept** or **huit** modify.

373. t is sounded in **au fait,** adv. But the t is silent in **fait,** subs., except at the end of the sentence:—

Dire à quelqu'un son fait, Je lui ai dit son fait, C'est un fait.
deer ă kehl kŭn̄ sōn̄ feht, zh' lŭ ee a dee sōn̄ feht, seh tun feht.

374. t is always silent in the conjunction **et,** even before a vowel.

375. In **vingt** the t is silent, but it is sounded in the nine compounds of that number:—

Vingt, vingt et un, vingt-deux, vingt-trois, vingt-quatre, vingt-
vĭn̄, vĭn̄ ta ŭn̄, vĭnt dĕū, vĭnt trwah, vĭnt kăt̄r', vĭnt
cinq, vingt-six, vingt-sept, vingt-huit, vingt-neuf.
sĭnk, vĭnt sees, vĭnt seht, vĭnt ŭ eet, vĭnt nuhf.

376. In **quatre-vingt,** and in its nineteen compounds, the g and t are invariably silent.

377. The t of **cent** is silent, except before a word multiplied by **cent,** and which begins with a vowel:—

Cent un, cent ou deux cents, cent équipages, cent hirondelles.
săn̄ ŭn̄, săn̄ oo dĕū săn̄, săn̄ ta kee păzh', săn̄ tee rōn̄ dehl'.

378. The t of **th** is sounded everywhere except in the three words:—

Goth, Ostrogoth, Wisigoth.
ḡo, ŏs trŏ ḡo, vee zee ḡo.

379. The t final preceded by **c** or **r** is not generally carried to the next word, and **c** and **r** make the connection. But **fort,** adv., generally carries its t.

Vous êtes fort obligeant.
voo zeht' fŏr tŏ blizhăn̄.

THEORY AND PRACTICE.

CONSONANT *T* (*continued*).

380. t is sounded in the following proper names: **A brecht, Alost, Anet, Anhalt, Apt, Ast, Ault, Austerlitz, Belfast, Belt, Bénédict, de Beust, Beyrout, Biarritz, Bombast, Brest, Bucharest, Christ, Crevelt, Danet, Duchapt, Dudouyt, Erfurt, Ernest, Faust, Hertz, Huet, Japhet, Kant, Kent, Laufelt, Lot-et-Garonne, Liszt, Olmutz, Pilnitz, Saint-Just, Saint-Vaast, Schmitz, Sedlitz, Soult, Strélitz, Tot, Vouet.**

381. But t is silent in the terminations ault, aut (except in Ault), and at the end of the proper names below.

Albert, Albret, Achmet, Adrets, Antechrist, Azincourt, Bajazet, Belleforest, Belfort, Benoit, Bossuet, Brunehaut, Capet, Cauterets, Charles-Quint, Charost, Châtellerault, la Ciotat, Coblentz, Colbert, Cronstadt, d'Alembert, Dancourt, Darmstadt, Davoust, Domfront, Dubost, Dumont, l'Escaut, Forêts, Fouquet, Giroust, Givet, Guéret, Humboldt, Japet, Jésus-Christ, Josaphat, Jundt, Lorient, Maëstrickt, Mahomet, Marat, Marrast, Metz, Murat, Niort, Nourrit, Nuits, de Pradt, Prévost, Rambouillet, Rastadt, Rembrandt, Retz, Robert, Saint-Priest, Schelestadt, Seltz, Sixte-Quint, Talbot, Thiboust, Utrecht.

382. **Asthme** and **isthme** are pronounced *asm'*, *ism'*.

383. When t is doubled, the first is silent except in the following words which sound both t's: **Algarotti, allégretto, atticisme, attique, battologie, battologique, committimus, committitur, concetti, dilettanti, Donizetti, et tutti quanti, Gambetta, guttifères, guttural, gutturo, in petto, intermittence, intermittent, quintetti, quintetto, vendetta, Viotti.**

THEORY AND PRACTICE.

CONSONANT V, AND W.

384. The French **v** is never doubled, never final, and never varies in its pronunciation.

385. **W** belongs to foreign words. We call it *double vuh*. It is pronounced as **v**,—

1°. In all German, Swede, Russian, Polish, &c., names:—

La Norwège, la Dwina, Wurtzbourg, Brunswick, Weber, &c.
là nŏr vehzh, là dvee nă, vürz boor, bōñs veek, va behr.

2°. In a few English words, especially when it is not preceded by a vowel:—

Cromwell, un wagon, un warrant.
krŏm vehl, ŭñ vă gōñ, ŭñ vă rañ.

386. **w** has the value of **ou** (oo in too), in English and Flemish words:—

Les Whigs, Longwy, whist.
la oo eeg, lōñg oo ee, oo eest.

387. In **Zwingle**, it is sounded **u**.

388. **w** is pronounced like **f** (*fuh*) at the end of Russian names:—

Mer d'Azow, Romanow.
mehr dă zof, rŏ mă nŏf.

389. **ow** final is sounded **o**:—

Flotow, Bulow.
flŏ to, bŭ lo.

390. **Newton, Washington, Warwick, Law, New York, cowpox,** are pronounced *neuton, vasinkton, varvic, lâ, neu york, côpox*.

CONSONANT X.

391. **Xerxès** is pronounced *gzercès*, and **Don Quixote**, *don quichotte*.

392. **x** final is carried to the next word, with the **z** sound, in the following cases:—

1°. From the article **aux**: **aux abonnés, aux horticulteurs.**

2°. From a noun to its adjective: **cheveux épars, chevaux alertes.**

3°. From an adjective to its substantive: **affreux état.**

4°. From **peux** and **veux**: tu peux écrire, je veux y aller.

5°. In poetry whenever euphony requires it.

393. **x** final and sounded is always articulated like **ks**.

THEORY AND PRACTICE.

CONSONANT X (*continued*).

394. x is articulated like ks in the terminations ax, ex, ix, ox, ux, yx, inx, ynx, when they are preceded by a consonant:

Borax, codex, préfix, Fox, Pollux, onyx, sphinx, lynx.
bŏ răks, kŏ dehks, pra feeks, fŏks,   pŏ lŭks, ŏ neeks,   sfĩnks,   lĩnks.

395. **Béatrix, coccyx, Cadix, Chastellux,** are pronounced *béatris, coccis, cadis, châtlû*.

396. In **crucifix, perdrix, prix,** and all the words ending in **flux**, the x is mute. It is also mute when it follows a consonant or several vowels: **Bordeaux, choux, Crémieux, Gréoulx,** &c.

CONSONANT Z.

397. z final in common words is silent, but may be carried to the next word beginning with a vowel.

398. z final in proper names, and in a few words of foreign origin, is sounded *zuh*, after a, i, o, u: **Achaz, Alcaniz.**

But z assumes the sound *suh* (as s in *so*) after e or any consonant: **Alvarez, Fritz, Metz, Retz,** pronounced *Alvarès, frits, Mès, Rès*. However, in **Suez** and **Séez,** z retains its proper sound.

399. z is always silent in **riz** and **nez**, even before a vowel. It is not sounded in the following words except before a vowel: **assez, biez, chez, lez, recez, rez, rez-de-chaussée, sonnez** (*subs.*).

z is also silent in the following proper names: **Cayz, Duez, Dumouriez, Duprez, Forez, Géruzez, Lainez, le Lez, les Natchez, Plessis-lez-Tours, Denis-lez-Paris.**

In the terminations of the second person plural of verbs z is silent except before a vowel.

400. z double, in a few words from the Italian language, is generally pronounced as single. Some persons, however, pronounce the first z as *d*, the second z, Italian fashion; a pedantic and affected pronunciation, which we do not recommend.

CONSONANTS.

PRACTICE.

FORTY-FIFTH EXERCISE. *Quarante-cinquième exercice.*

Une razzia, ŭn' ră zee ă.	a razzia.	Despréaux, da pra o.	Despreaux.
des lazzi, da lă zee.	some lazzi.	Bruix, brŭ ee.	Bruix.
Vélasquez, va lăs kehs.	Velasquez.	Vauxcelles, vo ksehl'.	Vauxcelles.
Lola Montez, lŏ lă mōn tehs.	Lola Montez.	Alexandre, ă lehk sān dr'.	Alexander.
six amis, see ză mee.	six friends.	Dombrowski, dōn brŏs kee.	Dombrowski.
trente-six tables, trānt' see tăbl'.	thirty-six [tables.	Witikind, vee tee kīnd.	Witikind.
page dix, păzh' dees.	tenth page.	Waterloo, vă tehr lo.	Waterloo.
deux enfants, deū zān fān.	two children.	Mourawief, moo ră vee ehf.	Mourawief.
deux livres, deū leevr'.	two pounds.	Thibault, tee bo.	Thibault.
ex-député, ehks da pŭ ta.	ex-deputy.	Perrault, peh ro.	Perrault.
Tallemand des Réaux, tăl' mān da ra o.	Talle- [mand des Reaux.	Saint-Genest, sīn zh' neh.	Saint-Genest.
Meaux, mo.	Meaux.	Brunehaut, brŭ nuh o.	Brunehaut.
Lecouteulx, luh koo teū.	Lecouteulx.	Tilsitt, Judith, teel seet, zhŭ deet.	Tilsitt, Judith.

ă, as; ah, äh, father; uh, ermine; ĕ or ', move; a, late; eh, met; ēh, there; ee, police; ŏ, nor; o, also; ō, no; ŭ, constitution; eū, first; oo, too; ān, want; īn, Yankee; ōn, don't; ūn, grunt; weh, wear; wah, water; ḡ, go; zh, glazier; ḡn, singing; ȳ, yes.

APPENDIX.

JOURS DE LA SEMAINE.   *Days of the Week.*
zhoor   duh   lă   s'   mehn'.

Dimanche, Sunday.
dee mănsh'.

Mercredi, Jeudi, Wednesday, [Thursday.
mehr kruh dee, zhēū dee.

Lundi, Mardi, Monday, Tuesday.
lŭñ dee, măr dee.

Vendredi, Samedi, Friday, Sat- [urday.
văñ druh dee, săm' dee.

SAISONS DE L'ANNÉE.   *Seasons of the Year.*
seh   zōñ   d'   l'ă   na.

Le printemps, Spring.
luh priñ tăñ.

L'automne, Autumn.
lo tŏn'.

L'été, Summer.
la ta.

L'hiver, Winter.
lee vehr.

MOIS DE L'ANNÉE.   *Months of the Year.*
mwah   d'   l'ă   na.

Janvier, January.
zhăñ vee a.

Juillet, July.
zhŭ ee yeh.

Février, February.
fa vree a.

Août, August.
oo.

Mars, March.
marss.

Septembre, September.
sehp tăñbr'.

Avril, April.
ă vreel.

Octobre, October.
ŏk tŏbr'.

Mai, May.
meh.

Novembre, November.
nŏ văñbr'.

Juin, June.
zhŭ iñ.

Décembre, December.
da săñbr'.

NOMBRES.   *Numbers.*
nōñ   br'.

Un, une, One.
ŭñ, ŭnŏ.

Trois, Three.
trwah.

Deux, Two.
dŏū.

Quatre, Four.
kătr'.

FRENCH PRONUNCIATION.

Cinq, sĭnk.	Five.
Six, seess.	Six.
Sept, seht.	Seven.
Huit, ŭ eet.	Eight.
Neuf, nuhf.	Nine.
Dix, deess.	Ten.
Onze, ōnz'.	Eleven.
Douze, dooz'.	Twelve.
Treize, trehz'.	Thirteen.
Quatorze, kă torz'.	Fourteen.
Quinze, kĭnz'.	Fifteen.
Seize, sehz'.	Sixteen.
Dix-sept, deess seht.	Seventeen.
Dix-huit, dee zŭ eet.	Eighteen.
Dix-neuf, deez nuhf.	Nineteen.
Vingt, vĭn.	Twenty.
Vingt et un, vĭn ta ŭn.	Twenty-one.
Vingt-deux, vĭnt dēu.	Twenty-two.
Vingt-trois, vĭnt trwah.	Twenty-three.
Vingt-quatre, vĭnt kătr'.	Twenty-four.
Vingt-cinq, vĭnt sĭnk.	Twenty-five.
Vingt-six, vĭnt seess.	Twenty-six.
Vingt-sept, vĭnt seht.	Twenty-seven.
Vingt-huit, vĭnt ŭ eet.	Twenty-eight.
Vingt-neuf, vĭnt nuhf.	Twenty-nine.
Trente, trănt'.	Thirty.
Trente et un, trăn ta ŭn.	Thirty-one.
Trente-deux, trănt' dēu.	Thirty-two.
Trente-trois, trănt' trwah.	Thirty-three.
Trente-quatre, trănt' kătr'.	Thirty-four.
Trente-cinq, trănt' sĭnk.	Thirty-five.
Trente-six, trănt' seess.	Thirty-six.
Trente-sept, trănt' seht.	Thirty-seven.
Trente-huit, trănt' ŭ eet.	Thirty-eight.
Trente-neuf, trănt' nuhf.	Thirty-nine.
Quarante, kă rănt'.	Forty.
Quarante et un, kă răn t'a ŭn.	Forty-one.
Quarante-deux, kă rănt' dēu.	Forty-two.
Quarante-trois, kă rănt' trwah.	Forty-three.
Quarante-quatre, kă rănt' kă tr'.	Forty-four.
Quarante-cinq, kă rănt' sĭnk.	Forty-five.
Quarante-six, kă rănt' seess.	Forty-six.
Quarante-sept, kă rănt' seht.	Forty-seven.
Quarante-huit, kă rănt' ŭ eet.	Forty-eight.

APPENDIX. 129

Quarante-neuf,	Forty-nine.	Soixante-dix,	Seventy.
kă rănt' nuhf.		sweh sănt' deess.	
Cinquante,	Fifty.	Soixante et onze,	Seventy-one.
sĭn kănt'.		sweh sănt' a ōnz'.	
Cinquante et un,	Fifty-one.	Soixante-douze,	Seventy-two.
sĭn kănt' a ūn.		sweh sănt' dooz'.	
Cinquante-deux,	Fifty-two.	Soixante-treize,	Seventy-three.
sĭn kănt' dēū.		sweh sănt' trehz'. [four.	
Cinquante-trois,	Fifty-three.	Soixante-quatorze, Seventy-	
sĭn kănt' trwah.		sweh sănt' kă torz'.	
Cinquante-quatre,	Fifty-four.	Soixante-quinze,	Seventy-five.
sĭn kănt' kătr'.		sweh sănt' kĭnz'.	
Cinquante-cinq,	Fifty-five.	Soixante-seize,	Seventy-six.
sĭn kănt' sĭnk.		sweh sănt' sehz'. [seven.	
Cinquante-six,	Fifty-six.	Soixante-dix-sept, Seventy-	
sĭn kănt' seess.		sweh sănt' deess seht. [eight.	
Cinquante-sept,	Fifty-seven.	Soixante-dix-huit, Seventy-	
sĭn kănt' seht.		sweh sănt' dee zū eet. [nine.	
Cinquante-huit,	Fifty-eight.	Soixante-dix-neuf, Seventy-	
sĭn kănt' ū eet.		sweh sănt' deez nuhf.	
Cinquante-neuf,	Fifty-nine.	Quatre-vingt,	Eighty.
sĭn kănt' nuhf.		kătr' vĭn.	
Soixante,	Sixty.	Quatre-vingt-un,	Eighty-one.
sweh sănt'.		kătr' vĭn ūn.	
Soixante et un,	Sixty-one.	Quatre-vingt-deux, Eighty-two.	
sweh sănt' a ūn.		kătr' vĭn dēū.	
Soixante-deux,	Sixty-two.	Quatre-vingt-trois, eighty-three.	
sweh sănt' dēū.		kătr' vĭn trwah. [four.	
Soixante-trois,	Sixty-three.	Quatre-vingt-quatre, Eighty-	
sweh sănt' trwah.		kătr' vĭn kătr'.	
Soixante-quatre,	Sixty-four.	Quatre-vingt-cinq, Eighty-five.	
sweh sănt' kătr'.		kătr' vĭn sĭnk.	
Soixante-cinq,	Sixty-five.	Quatre-vingt-six, Eighty-six.	
sweh sănt' sĭnk.		kătr' vĭn seess.	
Soixante-six,	Sixty-six.	Quatre-vingt-sept, eighty-seven.	
sweh sănt' seess.		kătr' vĭn seht.	
Soixante-sept,	Sixty-seven.	Quatre-vingt-huit, Eighty-eight.	
sweh sănt' seht.		kătr' vĭn ū eet.	
Soixante-huit,	Sixty-eight.	Quatre-vingt-neuf, Eighty-nine.	
sweh sănt' ū eet.		kătr' vĭn nuhf.	
Soixante-neuf,	Sixty-nine.	Quatre-vingt-dix,	Ninety.
sweh sănt' nuhf.		kătr' vĭn deess.	

Quatre-vingt-onze, Ninety-one.
kătr' viñ ōñz'.

Quatre-vingt-douze, Ninety-[two.
kătr' viñ dooz'.

Quatre-vingt-treize, Ninety-[three.
kătr' viñ trehz'.

Quatre-vingt-quatorze, Ninety-[four.
kătr' viñ kă torz'.

Quatre-vingt-quinze, Ninety-[five.
kătr' viñ kiñz'.

Quatre-vingt-seize, Ninety-six.
kătr' viñ sehz'.

Quatre-vingt-dix-sept, Ninety-[seven.
kătr' viñ deess seht.

Quatre-vingt-dix-huit, Ninety-[eight.
kătr' viñ dee zŭ eet.

Quatre-vingt-dix-neuf, Ninety-[nine.
kătr' viñ deez nuhf.

Cent, Cent un, &c., One hun-[dred, One hundred and one, &c.
sāñ, sāñ ūñ.

CONJUGATION OF THE AUXILIARY VERB
AVOIR, to have.
ă vwehr.

Infinitif Présent, **Avoir.**
iñ fee nee teef pra zāñ, ă vwehr.

Participe Présent, **Ayant.**
păr tee seep' pra zāñ, eh yāñ.

Composé, **Ayant eu.**
kōñ pŏ sa, eh yāñ tŭ.

Passé, **Avoir eu.**
pah sa. ă vwehr tŭ.

Passé, **Eu, eue, eus, eues.**
pah sa. ŭ, ŭ, ŭ, ŭ.

INDICATIF.
iñ dee kă teef.

TEMPS SIMPLES.
tāñ siñ pl'.

Présent.
pra zāñ.

J'ai.
zha.

tu as.
tŭ ă.

il a.
eel ă.

nous avons.
noo ză vōñ.

vous avez.
voo ză va.

ils ont.
eel zōñ.

TEMPS COMPOSÉS.
tāñ kōñ pŏ sa,

Passé indéfini.
pah sa iñ da fee nee.

J'ai eu.
zha ŭ.

tu as eu.
tŭ ă zŭ.

il a eu.
eel ă ŭ.

nous avons eu.
noo ză vōñ zŭ.

vous avez eu.
voo ză va zŭ.

ils ont eu.
eel zōñ tŭ.

Imparfait.
ĭn păr feh.

J'avais.
zhă veh.
tu avais.
tŭ ă veh.
il avait.
eel ă veh.
nous avions.
noo ză vee ōn.
vous aviez.
voo ză vee a.
ils avaient.
eel ză vĕh.

Passé défini.
pah sa da fee nee.

J'eus.
zhŭ.
tu eus.
tŭ ŭ.
il eut.
eel ŭ.
nous eûmes.
noo zŭm'.
vous eûtes.
voo zŭt'.
ils eurent.
eel zŭr'.

Futur simple.
fŭ tŭr sĭn pl'.

J'aurai.
zhŏ ra.
tu auras.
tŭ ŏ ră.
il aura.
eel ŏ ră.
nous aurons.
noo zŏ rōn.
vous aurez.
voo zŏ ra.
ils auront.
eel zŏ rōn.

Plus-que-parfait.
plŭss kuh păr feh.

J'avais eu.
zhă veh zŭ.
tu avais eu.
tŭ ă veh zŭ.
il avait eu.
eel ă veh tŭ.
nous avions eu.
noo ză vee ōn zŭ.
vous aviez eu.
voo ză vee a zŭ.
ils avaient eu.
eel za vĕh tŭ.

Passé antérieur.
pah sa ān ta ree uhr.

J'eus eu.
zhŭ zŭ.
tu eus eu.
tŭ ŭ zŭ.
il eut eu.
eel ŭ tŭ.
nous eûmes eu.
noo zŭm' zŭ.
vous eûtes eu.
voo zŭt' zŭ.
ils eurent eu.
eel zŭr' tŭ.

Futur antérieur.
fŭ tŭr ān ta ree uhr.

J'aurai eu.
zhŏ ra ŭ.
tu auras eu.
tŭ ŏ ră zŭ.
il aura eu.
eel ŏ ră ŭ.
nous aurons eu.
noo zŏ rōn zŭ.
vous aurez eu.
voo zŏ ra zŭ.
ils auront eu.
eel zŏ rōn tŭ.

CONDITIONNEL.
kŏn dee see ŏ nehl.

| *Présent.* | *Passé.* |
pra zān.	pah sa.
J'aurais.	J'aurais eu.
zhŏ reh.	zhŏ reh zŭ.
tu aurais.	tu aurais eu.
tŭ ŏ reh.	tŭ ŏ reh zŭ.
il aurait.	il aurait eu.
eel ŏ reh.	eel ŏ reh tŭ.
nous aurions.	nous aurions eu.
noo zŏ ree ŏn.	noo zŏ ree ŏn zŭ.
vous auriez.	vous auriez eu.
voo zŏ ree a.	voo zŏ ree a zŭ.
ils auraient.	ils auraient eu.
eel zŏ rēh.	eel zŏ rēh tŭ.

IMPÉRATIF.
īn pa rŭ teef

| Aie. | ayez. |
a.	eh ya.
qu'il ait.	qu'ils aient.
keel eh.	keel zēh.
ayons.	
eh yŏn.	

SUBJONCTIF.
sŭb zhŏnk teef.

| *Présent.* | *Passé.* |
pra zān.	pah sa.
Que j'aie.	Que j'aie eu.
kuh zha.	kuh zha ŭ.
que tu aies.	que tu aies eu.
kuh tŭ eh.	kuh tŭ eh zŭ.
qu'il ait.	qu'il ait eu.
keel eh.	keel eh tŭ.
que nous ayons.	que nous ayons eu.
kuh noo zeh yŏn.	kuh noo eh yŏn zŭ.
que vous ayez.	que vous ayez eu.
kuh voo zeh ya.	kuh voo zeh ya zŭ.
qu'ils aient.	qu'ils aient eu.
keel zēh.	keel zēh tŭ.

Imparfait.
ĩn păr feh.

Que j'eusse.
kuh zhüss'.
que tu eusses.
huh tü üss'.
qu'il eût.
keel ü.
que nous eussions.
kuh noo zü see ōn.
que vous eussiez.
kuh voo zü see a.
qu'ils eussent.
keel züss'.

Plus-que-parfait.
plüss kuh păr feh.

Que j'eusse eu.
huh zhüss ü.
que tu eusses eu.
kuh tü üss' zü.
qu'il eût eu.
keel ü tü.
que nous eussions eu.
kuh noo zü see ōn zü.
que vous eussiez eu.
kuh voo zü see a zü.
qu'ils eussent eu.
keel züss tü.

CONJUGATION OF THE AUXILIARY VERB ÊTRE, to be.
ēhtr'.

Infinitif Présent, **Être.**
ětr'.
Participe Présent, **Étant.**
a tăn.
Composé, **Ayant été.**
eh yăn ta ta.

Passé, **Avoir été.**
ă vwher a ta.
Passé, **Été.**
a ta.

INDICATIF.

Présent.

Je suis.
zhuh sü ee.
tu es.
tü eh.
il est.
eel eh.
nous sommes.
noo sŏm'.
vous êtes.
voo zěht'.
ils sont.
eel sōn.

Passé indéfini.

J'ai été.
zha a ta.
tu as été.
tü ă za ta.
il a été.
eel ă a ta.
nous avons été.
noo ză vōn za ta.
vous avez été.
voo ză va za ta.
ils ont été.
eel zōn ta ta.

Imparfait.

J'étais.
zha teh.
tu étais.
tü a teh.
il était.
eel a teh.
nous étions.
noo za tee ŏn.
vous étiez.
voo za tee a.
ils étaient.
eel za tĕh.

Passé défini.

Je fus.
zhuh fü.
tu fus.
tü fü.
il fut.
eel fü.
nous fûmes.
noo füm'.
vous fûtes.
voo füt'.
ils furent.
eel für'.

Futur simple.

Je serai.
zhuh s' ra.
tu seras.
tü s' rä.
il sera.
eel s' rä.
nous serons.
noo s' rŏn.
vous serez.
voo s' ra.
ils seront.
eel s' rŏn.

Plus-que-parfait.

J'avais été.
zhă veh za ta.
tu avais été.
tü ă veh za ta.
il avait été.
eel ă veh ta ta.
nous avions été.
noo ză vee ŏn za ta.
vous aviez été.
voo ză vee a za ta.
ils avaient été.
eel ză vĕh ta ta.

Passé antérieur.

J'eus été.
zhü za ta.
tu eus été.
tü ü za ta.
il eut été.
eel ü ta ta.
nous eûmes été.
noo üm' za ta.
vous eûtes été.
voo züt' za ta.
ils eurent été.
eel zür' ta ta.

Futur antérieur.

J'aurai été.
zhŏ ra a ta.
tu auras été.
tü ŏ rä za ta.
il aura été.
ŏ rä a ta.
nous aurons été.
noo zŏ rŏn za ta.
vous aurez été.
voo zŏ ra za ta.
ils auront été.
eel zŏ rŏn ta ta.

CONDITIONNEL.

Présent.

Je serais.
zhuh s' reh.
tu serais.
tü s' reh.
il serait.
eel s' reh.
nous serions.
noo suh ree ōn.
vous seriez.
voo suh ree a.
ils seraient.
eel s' rĕh.

Passé.

J'aurais été.
zhŏ reh za ta.
tu aurais été.
tü ŏ reh za ta.
il aurait été.
eel ŏ reh ta ta.
nous aurions été.
noo zŏ ree ōn za ta.
vous auriez été.
voo zŏ ree a za ta.
ils auraient été.
eel zŏ rĕh ta ta.

IMPÉRATIF.

Sois.
sweh.
qu'il soit.
keel sweh.
soyons.
sweh yōn.

soyez.
sweh ya.
qu'ils soient.
keel swĕh.

SUBJONCTIF.

Présent.

Que je sois.
kuh zhuh sweh.
que tu sois.
kuh tü sweh.
qu'il soit.
keel sweh.
que nous soyons.
kuh noo sweh yōn.
que vous soyez.
kuh voo sweh ya.
qu'ils soient.
keel swĕh.

Passé.

Que j'aie été.
kuh zha a ta.
que tu aies été.
kuh tü eh za ta.
qu'il ait été.
keel eh ta ta.
que nous ayons été.
kuh noo zeh yōn za ta.
que vous ayez été.
kuh voo zeh ya za ta.
qu'ils aient été.
keel zeh ta ta.

Imparfait.

Que je fusse.
kuh zhuh füss'.
que tu fusses.
kuh tü füss'.
qu'il fût.
keel fü.
que nous fussions.
kuh noo füsee ōn.
que vous fussiez.
kuh voo fü see a.
qu'ils fussent.
keel füss'.

Plus-que-parfait.

Que j'eusse été.
kuh zhüss a ta.
que tu eusses été.
kuh tü üss za ta.
qu'il eût été.
keel ü ta ta.
que nous eussions été.
kuh noo zü see ōn za ta.
que vous eussiez été.
kuh voo zü see a za ta.
qu'ils eussent été.
keel züss ta ta.

FIRST CONJUGATION, VERB *TRAVAILLER*,
to work.   tră vă ya.

Infinitif Présent, **Travailler.**
     tră vă ya.
Participe Présent, **Travaillant.**
     tră vă yāṅ.
Composé,   Ayant travaillé.
     eh yāṅ tră vă ya.

Passé,   Avoir travaillé.
     ă vwehr tră vă ya.
Passé,   Travaillé.
     tră vă ya.

INDICATIF.

Présent.

Je travaille.
zh' tră văy'.
tu travailles.
tü tră văy'.
il travaille.
eel tră văy'.
nous travaillons.
noo tră vă yōn.
vous travaillez.
voo tră vă ya.
ils travaillent.
eel tră vay'.

Passé indéfini.

J'ai travaillé.
zha tră vă ya.
tu as travaillé.
tü ă tră vă ya.
il a travaillé.
eel ă tră vă ya.
nous avons travaillé.
noo ză vōn tră vă ya.
vous avez travaillé.
voo ză va tră vă ya.
ils ont travaillé.
eel zōn tră vă ya.

APPENDIX.

Imparfait.

Je travaillais.
zh' trä vă yeh.
tu travaillais.
tü trä vă yeh.
il travaillait.
eel trä vă yeh.
nous travaillions.
noo trä vă yee ōn.
vous travailliez.
voo trä vă yee a.
ils travaillaient.
eel trä vă yeh.

Passé défini.

Je travaillai.
zh' trä vă ya.
tu travaillas.
tü trä vă yă.
il travailla.
eel trä vă yă.
nous travaillâmes.
noo trä vă yăm'.
vous travaillâtes.
voo trä vă yăt'.
ils travaillèrent.
eel trä vă yōhr.

Futur simple.

Je travaillerai.
zh' trä văy' ra.
tu travailleras.
tü trä văy' ră.
il travaillera.
eel trä văy' ră.
nous travaillerons.
noo trä văy' rōn.
vous travaillerez.
voo trä văy' ra.
ils travailleront.
eel trä văy' rōn.

Plus-que-parfait.

J'avais travaillé.
zhă veh trä vă ya.
tu avais travaillé.
tü ă veh trä vă ya.
il avait travaillé.
eel ă veh trä vă ya.
nous avions travaillé.
noo ză vee ōn trä vă ya.
vous aviez travaillé.
voo ză vee a trä vă ya.
ils avaient travaillé.
eel ză veh   trä vă ya.

Passé antérieur.

J'eus travaillé.
zhü   trä vă ya.
tu eus travaillé.
tü ü trä vă ya.
il eut travaillé.
eel ü trä vă ya.
nous eûmes travaillé.
noo züm'   trä vă ya.
vous eûtes travaillé
voo züt'   trä vă ya.
ils eurent travaillé.
eel zür'   trä vă ya.

Futur antérieur.

J'aurai travaillé.
zhō ra trä vă ya.
tu auras travaillé.
tü ō ră trä vă ya.
il aura travaillé.
eel ō ră trä vă ya.
nous aurons travaillé.
noo zō rōn trä vă ya.
vous aurez travaillé.
voo zō ra trä vă ya.
ils auront travaillé.
eel zō rōn trä vă ya.

CONDITIONNEL.

Présent.

Je travaillerais.
zh' tră văy' reh.
tu travaillerais.
tü tră văy' reh.
il travaillerait.
eel tră văy' reh.
nous travaillerions.
noo tră vă yuh ree ōn.
vous travailleriez.
voo tră vă yuh ree a.
ils travailleraient.
eel tră văy' reh.

Passé.

J'aurais travaillé.
zhŏ reh tră vă ya.
tu aurais travaillé.
tü ŏ reh tră vă ya.
il aurait travaillé.
eel ŏ reh tră vă ya.
nous aurions travaillé.
noo zŏ ree ōn tră vă ya.
vous auriez travaillé.
voo zŏ ree a tră vă ya.
ils auraient travaillé.
eel zŏ reh tră vă ya.

IMPÉRATIF.

Travaille.
tră văy'.
qu'il travaille.
keel tră văy'.
travaillons.
tră vă yōn.

travaillez.
tră vă ya.
qu'ils travaillent.
keel tră văy'.

SUBJONCTIF.

Présent.

Que je travaille.
kuh zh' tră văy'.
que tu travailles.
kuh tü tră văy'.
qu'il travaille.
keel tră văy'.
que nous travaillions.
kuh noo tră vă yee ōn.
que vous travailliez.
kuh voo tră vă yee a.
qu'ils travaillent.
keel tră văy'.

Passé.

Que j'aie travaillé.
kuh zha tră vă ya.
que tu aies travaillé.
kuh tü eh tră vă ya.
qu'il ait travaillé.
keel eh tră vă ya.
que nous ayons travaillé.
kuh noo zeh yōn tră vă ya.
que vous ayez travaillé.
kuh voo zeh ya tră vă ya.
qu'ils aient travaillé.
keel zeh tră vă ya.

APPENDIX.

Imparfait.	*Plus-que-parfait.*
Que je travaillasse.	**Que j'eusse travaillé.**
kuh zh' tră vă yăss'.	kuh zhüss' tră vă ya.
que tu travaillasses.	que tu eusses travaillé.
kuh tu tră vă yăss'.	kuh tü üss' tră vă ya.
qu'il travaillât.	qu'il eût travaillé.
keel tră vă yă.	keel ü tră vă ya.
que nous travaillassions.	que nous eussions travaillé.
kuh noo tră vă yă see ōn.	kuh noo sü see ōn tră vă ya.
que vous travaillassiez.	que vous eussiez travaillé.
kuh voo tră vă yă see a.	kuh voo sü see a tră vă ya.
qu'ils travaillassent.	qu'ils eussent travaillé.
keel tră vă yăss'.	keel züss' tră vă ya.

REGULAR VERBS,—*EMPLOYER, to employ*, AND
ān plweh ya.
ESSAYER, to try.
a seh ya.

Infinitif Présent,	**Employer.**	**Essayer.**
	ān plweh ya.	a seh ya.
Participe Présent,	**Employant.**	**Essayant.**
	ān plweh yān.	a seh yān.
Passé,	**Employé.**	**Essayé.**
	ān plweh ya.	a seh ya.

INDICATIF.
Présent.

J'emploie.	**J'essaie.**
zhān plweh.	zha sa.
tu emploies.	tu essaies.
tü ān plweh.	tü a seh.
il emploie.	il essaie.
eel ān plweh.	eel a sa.
nous employons.	nous essayons.
noo zān plweh yōn.	noo za seh yōn.
vous employez.	vous essayez.
voo zān plweh ya.	voo za seh ya.
ils emploient.	ils essaient.
eel zān plweh.	eel za seh.

Imparfait.

J'employais. zhāṅ plweh yeh.	**J'essayais.** zha seh yeh.
tu employais. tü āṅ plweh yeh.	**tu essayais.** tü a seh yeh.
il employait. eel āṅ plweh yeh.	**il essayait.** eel a seh yeh.
nous employions. noo zāṅ plweh yee ōṅ.	**nous essayions.** noo za seh yee ōṅ.
vous employiez. voo zāṅ plweh yee a.	**vous essayiez.** voo za seh yee a.
ils employaient. eel zāṅ plweh yeh.	**ils essayaient.** eel za seh yeh.

Passé défini.

J'employai. zhāṅ plweh ya.	**J'essayai.** zha seh ya.
tu employas. tü āṅ plweh yă.	**tu essayas.** tü a seh yă.
il employa. eel āṅ plweh yă.	**il essaya.** eel a seh yă.
nous employâmes. noo zāṅ plweh yăm'.	**nous essayâmes.** noo za seh yăm'.
vous employâtes. voo zāṅ plweh yăt'.	**vous essayâtes.** voo za seh yăt'.
ils employèrent. eel zāṅ plweh yehr.	**ils essayèrent.** eel za seh yehr.

Futur simple.

J'emploierai. zhāṅ plweh ra.	**J'essaierai.** zha seh ra.
tu emploieras. tü āṅ plweh ră.	**tu essaieras.** tü a seh ră.
il emploiera. eel āṅ plweh ră.	**il essaiera.** eel a seh ră.
nous emploierons. noo zāṅ plweh rōṅ.	**nous essaierons.** noo za seh rōṅ.
vous emploierez. voo zāṅ plweh ra.	**vous essaierez.** voo za seh ra.
ils emploieront. eel zāṅ plweh rōṅ.	**ils essaieront.** eel za seh rōṅ.

CONDITIONNEL.
Présent.

J'emploierais.
zhān plweh reh.
tu emploierais.
tü ān plweh reh.
il emploierait.
eel ān plweh reh.
nous emploierions.
noo zān plweh ree ōn.
vous emploieriez.
voo zān plweh ree a.
ils emploieraient.
eel zān plweh rĕh.

J'essaierais.
zha seh reh.
tu essaierais.
tü a seh reh.
il essaierait.
eel a seh reh.
nous essaierions.
noo za seh ree ōn.
vous essaieriez.
voo za seh ree a.
ils essaieraient.
eel za seh rĕh.

IMPÉRATIF.

Emploie.
ān plweh.
qu'il emploie.
keel ān plweh.
employons.
ān plweh yōn.
employez.
ān plweh ya.
qu'ils emploient.
keel zān plweh.

Essaie.
a sa.
qu'il essaie.
keel a sa.
essayons.
a seh yōn.
essayez.
a seh ya.
qu'ils essaient.
keel za sĕh.

SUBJONCTIF.
Présent.

Que j'emploie.
kuh zhān plweh.
que tu emploies.
kuh tü āu plweh.
qu'il emploie.
keel āu plweh.
que nous employions.
kuh noo zān plweh yee ōn.
que vous employiez.
kuh voo zān plweh ya.
qu'ils emploient.
keel zān plweh.

Que j'essaie.
kah zha sa.
que tu essaies.
kuh tü a seh.
qu'il essaie.
keel a sa.
que nous essayions.
kuh noo za seh yee ōn.
que vous essayiez.
kuh voo za seh yee a.
qu'ils essaient.
keel za sĕh.

FRENCH PRONUNCIATION.

Imparfait.

Que j'employasse.
kuh zhāṅ plweh yăss'.

que tu employasses.
kuh tü āṅ plweh yăss'.

qu'il employât.
keel āṅ plweh yă.

que nous employassions.
kuh noo zāṅ plweh yă see ōṅ.

que vous employassiez.
kuh voo zāṅ plweh yă see a.

qu'ils employassent.
keel zāṅ plweh yăss'.

Que j'essayasse.
kuh zha seh yăss'.

que tu essayasses.
kuh tü a seh yăss'.

qu'il essayât.
keel a seh yă.

que nous essayassions.
kuh noo za seh yă see ōṅ.

que vous essayassiez.
kuh voo za seh yă see a.

qu'ils essayassent.
keel za seh yăss'.

REGULAR VERBS, — *ETUDIER*, to study, AND
a tü dee a.
ARGUER, to argue.
ăr gü a.

Infinitif Présent,	Etudier.	Arguer.
	a tü dee a.	ăr gü a.
Participe Present,	Etudiant.	Arguant.
	a tü dee āṅ.	ăr gü āṅ.
Passé,	Etudié.	Argué.
	a tü dee a.	ăr gü a.

INDICATIF.
Présent.

J'étudie.
zha tü dee.

tu étudies.
tü a tü dee.

il étudie.
eel a tü dee.

nous étudions.
noo za tü dee ōṅ.

vous étudiez.
voo za tü dee a.

ils étudient.
eel za tü dee.

J'arguë.
zhăr gü.

tu arguës.
tü ăr gü.

il arguë.
eel ăr gü.

nous arguons.
noo zăr gü ōṅ.

vous arguez.
voo zăr gü a.

ils arguënt.
eel zăr gü.

Imparfait.

J'étudiais.
zha tü dee eh.
tu étudiais.
tü a tü dee eh.
il étudiait.
eel a tü dee eh.
nous etudiions.
noo za tü dee yōñ.
vous etudiiez.
voo za tü dee ya.
ils étudiaient.
eel za tü dee eh.

J'arguais.
zhär gü eh.
tu arguais.
tü är gü eh.
il arguait.
eel är gü eh.
nous arguïons.
noo zär gü yōñ.
vous arguïez.
voo zär gü ya.
ils arguaient.
eel zär gü ōh.

Passé défini.

J'étudiai.
zha tü dee a.
tu étudias.
tü a tü dee ä.
il étudia.
eel a tü dee ä.
nous étudiâmes.
noo za tü dee äm'.
vous étudiâtes.
voo za tü dee ät'.
ils étudièrent.
eel za tü dee ōhr'.

J'arguai.
zhär gü a.
tu arguas.
tü är gü ä.
il argua.
eel är gü ä.
nous arguâmes.
noo zär gü äm'.
vous arguâtes.
voo zär gü ät'.
ils arguèrent.
eel zär gü ōhr'.

Futur simple.

J'étudierai.
zha tü dee ra.
tu étudieras.
tü a tü dee rä.
il étudiera.
eel a tü dee rä.
nous étudierons.
noo za tü dee rōñ.
vous étudierez.
voo za tü dee ra.
ils étudieront.
eel za tü dee rōñ.

J'arguërai.
zhär gü ra.
tu arguëras.
tü är gü rä.
il arguëra.
eel är gü rä.
nous arguërons.
noo zär gü rōñ.
vous arguërez.
voo zär gü ra.
ils arguëront.
eel zär gü rōñ.

CONDITIONNEL.
Présent.

J'étudierais.
zha tü dee reh.
tu étudierais.
tü a tü dee reh.
il étudierait.
eel a tü dee reh.
nous étudierions.
noo za tü dee ree ōn.
vous étudieriez.
voo za tü dee ree a.
ils étudieraient.
eel za tü dee reh.

J'arguërais.
zhär gü reh.
tu arguërais.
tü är gü reh.
il arguërait.
eel är gü reh.
nous arguërions.
noo zär gü ree ōn.
vous arguëriez.
voo zär gü ree a.
ils arguëraient.
eel zär gü rëh.

IMPÉRATIF.

Etudie.
a tü dee.
qu'il étudie.
keel a tü dee.
étudions.
a tü dee ōn.
étudiez.
a tü dee a.
qu'ils étudient.
keel za tü dee.

Arguë.
är gü.
qu'il arguë.
keel är gü.
arguons.
är gü ōn.
arguez.
är gü a.
qu'ils arguënt.
keel zär gü.

SUBJONCTIF.
Présent.

Que j'étudie.
kuh zha tü dee.
que tu étudies.
kuh tü a tü dee.
qu'il étudie.
keel a tü dee.
que nous étudiions.
kuh noo za tü dee yōn.
que vous étudiiez.
kuh voo za tü dee ya.
qu'ils étudient.
keel za tü dee.

Que j'arguë.
kuh zhär gü.
que tu arguës.
kuh tü är gü.
qu'il arguë.
keel är gü.
que nous arguïons.
kuh noo zär gü yōn.
que vous arguïez.
kuh voo zär gü ya.
qu'ils arguënt.
keel zär gü.

APPENDIX.

Imparfait.

Que j'étudiasse.	**Que j'arguasse.**
kuh zha tü dee ăss'.	kuh zhăr gü ăss'.
que tu étudiasses.	**que tu arguasses.**
kuh tü a tü dee ăss'.	kuh tü ăr gü ăss'.
qu'il étudiât.	**qu'il arguât.**
keel a tü dee ă.	keel ăr gü ă.
que nous étudiassions.	**que nous arguassions.**
kuh noo za tü dee ă see ōn.	kuh noo zăr gü ă see ōn.
que vous étudiassiez.	**que vous arguassiez.**
kuh voo za tü dee ă see ă.	kuh voo zăr gü ă see a.
qu'ils étudiassent.	**qu'ils arguassent.**
keel za tü dee ăss'.	keel zăr gü ăss'.

REGULAR VERBS,— *SUBSTITUER*, to *substitute*,
sübs tee tü a.
AND *JOUER*, to *play*.
zhoo a.

Infinitif Présent,	**Substituer.**	**Jouer.**
	sübs tee tü a.	zhoo a.
Participe Présent,	**Substituant.**	**Jouant.**
	sübs tee tü āṅ.	zhoo āṅ.
Passé,	**Substitué.**	**Joué.**
	sübs tee tü a.	zhoo a.

INDICATIF.

Présent.

Je substitue.	**Je joue.**
zhuh sübs tee tü.	zhuh zhoo.
tu substitues.	**tu joues.**
tü sübs tee tü.	tü zhoo.
il substitue.	**ils joue.**
eel sübs tee tü.	eel zhoo.
nous substituons.	**nous jouons.**
noo sübs tee tü ōn.	noo zhoo ōn.
vous substituez.	**vous jouez.**
voo sübs tee tü a.	voo zhoo a.
ils substituent.	**ils jouent.**
eel sübs tee tü.	eel zhoo.

Imparfait.

Je substituais.
zhuh sübs tee tü eh.
tu substituais.
tü sübs tee tü eh.
il substituait.
eel sübs tee tü eh.
nous substituïons.
noo sübs tee tü yōn.
vous substituïez.
voo sübs tee tü ya.
ils substituaient.
eel sübs tee tü äh.

Je jouais.
zhuh zhoo eh.
tu jouais.
tü zhoo eh.
il jouait.
eel zhoo eh.
nous jouïons.
noo zhoo yōn.
vous jouïez.
voo zhoo ya.
ils jouaient.
eel zhoo äh.

Passé défini.

Je substituai.
zhuh sübs tee tü a.
tu substituas.
tü sübs tee tü ă.
il substitua.
eel sübs tee tü ă.
nous substituâmes.
noo sübs tee tu ăm'.
vous substituâtes.
voo sübs tee tü ăt'.
ils substituèrent.
eel sübs tee tü ähr.

Je jouai.
zhuh zhoo a.
tu jouas.
tü zhoo ă.
il joua.
eel zhoo ă.
nous jouâmes.
noo zhoo ăm'.
vous jouâtes.
voo zhoo ăt'.
ils jouèrent.
eel zhoo ähr.

Futur simple.

Je substituerai.
zhuh sübs tee tü ra.
tu substitueras.
tü sübs tee tü ră.
il substituera.
eel sübs tee tü ră.
nous substituerons.
noo sübs tee tü rōn.
vous substituerez.
voo sübs tee tü ra.
ils substitueront.
eel sübs tee tü rōn.

Je jouerai.
zhuh zhoo ra.
tu joueras.
tü zhoo ră.
il jouera.
eel zhoo ră.
nous jouerons.
noo zhoo rōn.
vous jouerez.
voo zhoo ra.
ils joueront.
eel zhoo rōn.

CONDITIONNEL.
Présent.

Je substituerais.
zhuh sübs tee tü reh.
tu substituerais.
tü sübs tee tü reh.
il substituerait.
eel sübs tee tü reh.
nous substituerions.
noo sübs tee tü ree õn.
vous substitueriez.
voo sübs tee tü ree a.
ils substitueraient.
eel sübs tee tü reh.

Je jouerais.
zhuh zhoo reh.
tu jouerais.
tü zhoo reh.
il jouerait.
eel zhoo reh.
nous jouerions.
noo zhoo ree õn.
vous joueriez.
voo zhoo ree a.
ils joueraient.
eel zhoo rěh.

IMPÉRATIF.

Substitue.
sübs tee tü.
qu'il substitue.
keel sübs tee tü.
substituons.
sübs tee tü õn.
substituez.
sübs tee tü a.
qu'ils substituent.
keel sübs tee tü.

Joue.
zhoo.
qu'il joue.
keel zhoo.
jouons.
zhoo õn.
jouez.
zhoo a.
qu'ils jouent.
keel zhoo.

SUBJONCTIF.
Présent.

Que je substitue.
küh zhuh sübs tee tü.
que tu substitues.
kuh tü subs tee tü.
qu'il substitue.
keel sübs tee tü.
que nous substituïons.
kuh noo sübs tee tü yõn.
que vous substituïez.
kuh voo sübs tee tü ya.
qu'ils substituent.
keel sübs tee tü.

Que je joue.
kuh zhuh zhoo.
que tu joues.
kuh tü zhoo.
qu'il joue.
keel zhoo.
que nous jouïons.
kuh noo zhoo yõn.
que vous jouïez.
kuh voo zhoo ya.
qu'ils jouent.
keel zhoo.

Imparfait.

Que je substituasse.	**Que je jouasse.**
kuh zhuh sŭbs tee tŭ ăss'.	kuh zhuh zhoo ăss'.
que tu substituasses.	que tu jouasses.
kuh tŭ sŭbs tee tŭ ăss'.	kuh tŭ zhoo ăss'.
qu'il substituât.	qu'il jouât.
keel sŭbs tee tŭ ă.	keel zhoo ă.
que nous substituassions.	que nous jouassions.
kuh noo sŭbs tee tŭ ă see ōn.	kuh noo zhoo ă see ōn.
que vous substituassiez.	que vous jouassiez.
kuh voo sŭbs tee tŭ ă see a.	kuh voo zhoo ă see a.
qu'ils substituassent.	qu'ils jouassent.
keel sŭbs tee tŭ ăss'.	keel zhoo ăss'.

REFLECTIVE VERB *S'EN ALLER*, to go away.
sān nă la.

Infinitif Présent,	S'en aller.	*Passé,*	S'en être allé.
	sān nă la.		sān nĕhtr' ă la.
Participe Présent,	S'en allant.	*Passé,*	Allé.
	sān nă lān.		ă la.
Composé,	S'en étant allé.		
	sān na tān tă la.		

INDICATIF.

Temps simples.	Temps composés.
Présent.	*Passé indéfini.*
Je m'en vais.	**Je m'en suis allé.**
zh' mān veh.	zh' mān sŭ ee ză la.
tu t'en vas.	tu t'en es allé.
tŭ tān vă.	tŭ tān neh ză la.
il s'en va.	il s'en est allé.
eel sān vă.	eel sān neh tă la.
nous nous en allons.	nous nous en sommes allés.
noo noo zān nă lōn.	noo noo zān sŏm' ză la.
vous vous en allez.	vous vous en êtes allés.
voo voo zan nă la.	voo voo zān nĕht ză la.
ils s'en vont.	ils s'en sont allés.
eel sān vōn.	eel sān sōn tă la.

Imparfait.

Je m'en allais.
zh' māṅ nă leh.
tu t'en allais.
tü tāṅ nă leh.
il s'en allait.
eel sāṅ nă leh.
nous nous en allions.
noo noo zāṅ nă lee ōṅ.
vous vous en alliez.
voo voo zāṅ nă lee a.
ils s'en allaient.
eel sāṅ nă leh.

Passé défini.

Je m'en allai.
zh' māṅ nă la.
tu t'en allas.
tü tāṅ nă lă.
il s'en alla.
eel sāṅ nă lă.
nous nous en allâmes.
noo noo zāṅ nă lăm'.
vous vous en allâtes.
voo voo zāṅ nă lăt'.
ils s'en allèrent.
eel sāṅ nă lāhr'.

Futur simple.

Je m'en irai.
zh' māṅ nee ra.
tu t'en iras.
tü tāṅ nee ră.
il s'en ira.
eel sāṅ nee ra.
nous nous en irons.
noo noo zāṅ nee rōṅ.
vous vous en irez.
voo voo zāṅ nee ra.
ils s'en iront.
eel sāṅ nee rōṅ.

Plus-que-parfait.

Je m'en étais allé.
zh' māṅ na teh ză la.
tu t'en étais allé.
tü tāṅ na teh ză la.
il s'en était allé.
eel sāṅ na teh tă la.
nous nous en étions allés.
noo noo zāṅ na tee ōṅ ză la.
vous vous en étiez allés.
voo voo zāṅ na tee a ză la.
ils s'en étaient allés.
eel sāṅ na teh tă la.

Passé antérieur.

Je m'en fus allé.
zh' māṅ fü ză la.
tu t'en fus allé.
tü tāṅ fü ză la.
il s'en fut allé.
eel sāṅ fü tă la.
nous nous en fûmes allés.
noo noo zāṅ füm' ză la.
vous vous en fûtes allés.
voo voo zāṅ füt' ză la.
ils s'en furent allés.
eel sāṅ für' tă la.

Futur antérieur.

Je m'en serai allé.
zh' māṅ s' ra ă la.
tu t'en seras allé.
tü tan s' ră ză la.
il s'en sera allé.
eel sāṅ s' ră ă la.
nous nous en serons allés.
noo noo zāṅ s' rōṅ ză la.
vous vous en serez allés.
voo voo zāṅ s' ra ză la.
ils s'en seront allés.
eel sāṅ s' rōṅ tă la.

CONDITIONNEL.

Présent.

Je m'en irais.
zh' mān nee reh.

tu t'en irais.
tū tān nee reh.

il s'en irait.
eel sān nee reh.

nous nous en irions.
noo noo zān nee ree ōn.

vous vous en iriez.
voo voo zān nee ree a.

ils s'en iraient.
eel sān nee rŏh.

Passé.

Je m'en serais allé.
zh' mān s' reh ză la.

tu t'en serais allé.
tū tān s' reh ză la.

il s'en serait allé.
eel sān s' reh tă la.

nous nous en serions allés.
noo noo zān suh ree ōn ză la.

vous vous en seriez allés.
voo voo zān suh reĕ a ză la.

ils s'en seraient allés.
eel sān s' rŏh tă la.

IMPÉRATIF.

Va-t'en.
vă tān.

qu'il s'en aille.
keel sān năhy'.

allons-nous-en.
ă' lōn noo zān.

allez-vous-en.
ă la voo zān.

qu'ils s'en aillent.
keel sān năhy'.

SUBJONCTIF.

Présent.

Que je m'en aille.
kuh zh' mān năhy'.

que tu t'en ailles.
kuh tū tān năhy'.

qu'il s'en aille.
keel sān năhy'.

que nous nous en allions.
kuh noo noo zān nă lee ōn.

que vous vous en alliez.
kuh voo voo zān nă lee a.

qu'ils s'en aillent.
keel sān năhy'.

Passé.

Que je m'en sois allé.
kuh zh' mān sweh ză la.

que tu t'en sois allé.
kuh tū tān sweh ză la.

qu'il s'en soit allé.
keel sān sweh tă la.

que nous nous en soyons allés.
kuh noo noo zān sweh yōn ză la.

que vous vous en soyez allés.
kuh voo voo zān sweh ya ză la.

qu'ils s'en soient allés.
keel sān sweh tă la.

Imparfait.

Que je m'en allasse.
kuh zh' mān nă lăss'.
que tu t'en allasses.
kuh tū tān nă lăss'.
qu'il s'en allât.
keel sān nă lă.
que nous nous en allassions.
kuh noo noo zān nă lă see ōn.
que vous vous en allassiez.
kuh voo voo zāū nă lă see a.
qu'ils s'en allassent.
keel sān nă lăss'.

Plus-que-parfait.

Que je m'en fusse allé.
kuh zh' mān fūss' ă la.
que tu t'en fusses allé.
kuh tū tān fūss' ză la.
qu'il s'en fût allé.
keel sān fū tă la.
que nous nous en fussions allés.
kuh noo noo zān fū see ōn ză la.
que vous vous en fussiez allés.
kuh voo voo zāū fū see a ză la.
qu'ils s'en fussent allés.
keel sān fūss' tă la.

REFLECTIVE VERB *S'HABILLER, to dress one's-*
să bee ya.
self.

Infinitif Présent,	S'habiller. să bee ya.	*Passé,*	S'être habillé. sěhtr' ă bee ya.
Participe Présent,	S'habillant. să bee yān.	*Passé,*	Habillé. ă bee ya.
Composé,	S'étant habillé. sa tān tă bee ya.		

INDICATIF.

Présent.

Je m'habille.
zh' mă beey'.
tu t'habilles.
tū tă beey'.
il s'habille.
eel să beey'.
nous nous habillons.
noo noo ză bee yōn.
vous vous habillez.
voo voo ză bee ya.
ils s'habillent.
eel să beey'.

Passé indéfini.

Je me suis habillé.
zhuh m' sū ee ză bee ya.
tu t'es habillé.
tu teh ză bee ya.
il s'est habillé.
eel seh tă bee ya.
nous nous sommes habillés.
noo noo sŏm' ză bee ya.
vous vous êtes habillés.
voo voo sěht' ză bee ya.
ils se sont habillés.
eel suh sōn tă bee ya.

Imparfait.

Je m'habillais.
zh' mă bee yeh.
tu t'habillais.
tü tă bee yeh.
il s'habillait.
eel să bee yeh.
nous nous habillions.
noo noo ză bee yee ōn.
vous vous habilliez.
voo voo ză bee yee a.
ils s'habillaient.
eel să bee yŏh.

Passé défini.

Je m'habillai.
zh' mă bee ya.
tu t'habillas.
tü tă bee yă.
il s'habilla.
eel să bee yă.
nous nous habillâmes.
noo noo ză bee yăm'.
vous vous habillâtes.
voo voo ză bee yăt'.
ils s'habillèrent.
eel să bee yŏhr'.

Futur simple.

Je m'habillerai.
zh' mă beey' ra.
tu t'habilleras.
tü tă beey' ră.
il s'habillera.
eel să beey' ră.
nous nous habillerons.
noo noo ză beey' rōn.
vous vous habillerez.
voo voo ză beey' ra.
ils s'habilleront.
eel să beey' rōn.

Plus-que-parfait.

Je m'étais habillé.
zh' ma teh ză bee ya.
tu t'étais habillé.
tü ta teh ză bee ya.
il s'était habillé
eel sa teh tă bee ya.
nous nous étions habillés.
noo noo za tee ōn ză bee ya.
vous vous étiez habillés.
voo voo za tee a ză bee ya.
ils s'étaient habillés.
eel sa tŏh tă bee ya.

Passé antérieur.

Je me fus habillé.
zhuh m' fü ză bee ya.
tu te fus habillé.
tü t' fü ză bee ya.
il se fut habillé.
eel suh fü tă bee yă.
nous nous fûmes habillés.
noo noo füm' ză bee ya.
vous vous fûtes habillés.
voo voo füt' ză bee ya.
ils se furent habillés.
eel suh für' tă bee ya.

Futur antérieur.

Je me serai habillé.
zhuh m' s' ra ă bee ya.
tu te seras habillé.
tü t' s' ră ză bee ya.
il se sera habillé.
eel suh s' ră ă bee ya.
nous nous serons habillés.
noo noo s' rōn ză bee ya.
vous vous serez habillés.
voo voo s' ra ză bee ya.
ils se seront habillés.
eel suh s' rōn tă bee ya.

CONDITIONNEL.

Présent.

Je m'habillerais.
zh' mă beey' reh.
tu t'habillerais.
tü tă beey' reh.
il s'habillerait.
eel să beey' reh.
nous nous habillerions.
noo noo ză bee yuh ree ōn.
vous vous habilleriez.
voo voo ză bee yuh ree a.
ils s'habilleraient.
eel să beey' rĕh.

Passé.

Je me serais habillé.
zhuh m' s' reh ză bee ya.
tu te serais habillé.
tü t' s' reh ză bee ya.
il se serait habillé.
eel suh s' reh tă bee ya.
nous nous serions habillés.
noo noo suh ree ōn ză bee ya.
vous vous seriez habillés.
voo voo suh ree a ză bee ya.
ils se seraient habillés.
eel suh s' rĕh tă bee ya.

IMPÉRATIF.

Habille-toi.
ă beey' tweh.
qu'il s'habille.
keel să beey'.
habillons-nous.
ă bee yōn noo.

habillez-vous.
ă bee ya voo.
qu'ils s'habillent.
keel să beey'.

SUBJONCTIF.

Présent.

Que je m'habille.
kuh zh' mă beey'.
que tu t'habilles.
kuh tü tă beey'.
qu'il s'habille.
keel să beey'.
que nous nous habillions.
kuh noo noo ză bee yee ōn.
que vous vous habilliez.
kuh voo voo ză bee yee a.
qu'ils s'habillent.
keel să beey'.

Passé.

Que je me sois habillé.
kuh zh' muh sweh ză bee ya.
que tu te sois habillé.
kuh tü t' sweh ză bee ya'.
qu'il se soit habillé.
keel suh sweh tă bee ya.
que nous nous soyons habillés.
kuh noo noo sweh yōn ză bee ya.
que vous vous soyez habillés.
kuh voo voo sweh ya ză bee ya.
qu'ils se soient habillés.
keel suh sweh tă bee yă.

Imparfait.	*Plus-que-parfait.*
Que je m'habillasse.	Que je me fusse habillé.
kuh zh' mă bee yăss'.	kuh zh' muh füss' ă bee ya.
que tu t'habillasses.	que tu te fusses habillé.
kuh tü tă bee yăss'.	kuh tü t' füss' ză bee ya.
qu'il s'habillât.	qu'il se fût habillé.
keel să bee yă.	keel suh fü tă bee ya.
que nous nous habillassions.	que nous nous fussions habillés.
kuh noo noo ză bee yă see ōn.	kuh noo noo fü see ōn ză bee ya.
que vous vous habillassiez.	que vous vous fussiez habillés.
kuh voo voo ză bee ya see a.	kuh voo voo fü see a ză bee ya.
qu'ils s'habillassent.	qu'ils se fussent habillés.
keel să bee yăss'.	keel suh füss' tăbee ya.

REFLECTIVE VERBS,— *S'AGENOUILLER, to kneel*
săzh'ᵃ noo ya.

down, AND *S'ENNUYER, to be weary.*
săn nü ee ya.

Infinitif Présent,	S'agenouiller.	S'ennuyer.
	săzh' noo ya.	săn nü ee ya.
Participe Présent,	S'agenouillant.	S'ennuyant.
	săzh' noo yăn.	săn nü ee yăn.
Passé,	Agenouillé.	Ennuyé.
	ăzh' noo ya.	ăn nü ee ya.

INDICATIF.

Présent.

Je m'agenouille.	Je m'ennuie.
zh' măzh' nooy'.	zh' măn nü ee.
tu t'agenouilles.	tu t'ennuies.
tü tăzh' nooy'.	tü tăn nü ee.
il s'agenouille.	il s'ennuie.
eel săzh' nooy'.	eel săn nü ee.
nous nous agenouillons.	nous nous ennuyons.
noo noo zăzh' noo yōn.	noo noo zăn nü ee yōn.
vous vous agenouillez.	vous vous ennuyez.
voo voo săzh' noo ya.	voo voo săn nü ee ya.
ils s'agenouillent.	ils s'ennuient.
eel săzh' nooy'.	eel săn nü ee.

APPENDIX.

Imparfait.

Je m'agenouillais.
zh' măzh' noo yeh.
tu t'agenouillais.
tŭ tăzh' noo yeh.
il s'agenouillait.
eel săzh' noo yeh.
nous nous agenouillions.
noo   noo zăzh' noo yee ōn.
vous vous agenouilliez.
voo   voo zăzh' noo yee a.
ils s'agenouillaient.
eel săzh' noo   yĕh.

Je m'ennuyais.
zh' măn nŭ ee yeh.
tu t'ennuyais.
tŭ tăn nŭ ee yeh.
il s'ennuyait.
eel săn nŭ ee yeh.
nous nous ennuyions.
noo   noo zăn nŭ ee yee ōu.
vous vous ennuyiez.
voo   voo zăn nŭ ee yee a.
ils s'ennuyaient.
eel săn nŭ ee yeh.

Passé défini.

Je m'agenouillai.
zh' mazh' noo ya.
tu t'agenouillas.
tŭ tăzh noo yă.
il s'agenouilla.
eel săzh' noo yă.
nous nous agenouillâmes.
noo   noo zăzh' noo yăm'.
vous vous agenouillâtes.
voo   voo zăzh' noo yăt'.
ils s'agenouillèrent.
eel săzh' noo   yĕhr.

Je m'ennuyai.
zh' măn nŭ ee ya.
tu t'ennuyas.
tŭ tăn nŭ ee yă.
il s'ennuya.
eel săn nŭ ee yă.
nous nous ennuyâmes.
noo   noo zăn nŭ ee yăm'.
vous vous ennuyâtes.
voo   voo zăn nŭ ee yăt'.
ils s'ennuyèrent.
eel săn nŭ ee yĕhr'.

Futur simple.

Je m'agenouillerai.
zh' măzh'   nooy' ra.
tu t'agenouilleras.
tŭ tăzh' nooy' ră.
il s'agenouillera.
eel săzh' nooy' ră.
nous nous agenouillerons.
noo   noo zăzh' nooy' rōn.
vous vous agenouillerez.
voo   voo zăzh' nooy' ra.
ils s'agenouilleront.
eel săzh' nooy'   rōn.

Je m'ennuierai.
zh' măn nŭ ee ra.
tu t'ennuieras.
tŭ tăn nŭ ee ră.
il s'ennuiera.
eel săn nŭ ee ră.
nous nous ennuierons.
noo   noo zăn nŭ ee rōn.
vous vous ennuieres.
voo   voo zăn nŭ ee ra.
ils s'ennuieront.
eel săn nŭ ee rōn.

CONDITIONNEL.

Présent.

Je m'agenouillerais.
zh' măzh' nooy'   reh.
tu t'agenouillerais.
tŭ tăzh' nooy' reh.
il s'agenouillerait.
eel săzh' nooy' reh.
nous nous agenouillerions.
noo   noo zăzh' noo yuh ree ōn.
vous vous agenouilleriez.
voo   voo zăzh' noo yuh ree a.
ils s'agenouilleraient.
eel săzh' noor y' rĕh.

Je m'ennuierais.
zh' măn nŭ ee reh.
tu t'ennuierais.
tŭ tăn nŭ ee reh.
il s'ennuierait.
eel săn nŭ ee reh.
nous nous ennuierions.
noo   noo zăn nŭ ee ree ōn.
vous vous ennuieriez.
voo   voo zăn nŭ ee ree a.
ils s'ennuieraient.
eel săn nŭ ee rĕh.

IMPÉRATIF.

Agenouille-toi.
ăzh' nooy' tweh.
qu'il s'agenouille.
keel săzh' nooy'.
agenouillons-nous.
ăzh' noo yōn noo.
agenouillez-vous.
ăzh' noo ya voo.
qu'ils s'agenouillent.
keel săzh' nooy'.

Ennuie-toi.
ăn nŭ ee tweh.
qu'il s'ennuie.
keel săn nŭ ee.
ennuyons-nous.
ăn nŭ ee yōn noo.
ennuyez-vous.
ăn nŭ ee ya voo.
qu'ils s'ennuient.
keel san nŭ ee.

SUBJONCTIF.

Présent.

Que je m'agenouille.
kuh zh' măzh' nooy'.
que tu t'agenouilles.
kuh tŭ tăzh' nooy'.
qu'il s'agenouille.
keel săzh' nooy'.
que nous nous agenouillons.
kuh noo   noo zazh' noo yee ōn.
que vous vous agenouilliez.
kuh voo   voo zăzh' noo yee a.
qu'ils s'agenouillent.
keel săzh'   nooy'.

Que je m'ennuie.
kuh zh' măn nŭ ee.
que tu t'ennuies.
kuh tŭ tăn nŭ ee.
qu'il s'ennuie.
keel săn nŭ ee.
que nous nous ennuyions.
kuh noo   noo zăn nŭ ee yee ōn.
que vous vous ennuyiez.
kuh voo   voo zăn nŭ ee yee a.
qu'ils s'ennuient.
keel săn nŭ ee.

APPENDIX.

Imparfait.

Que je m'agenouillasse.
kuh zh' măzh' noo yăss'.
que tu t'agenouillasses.
kuh tū tăzh' noo yass'.
qu'il s'agenouillât.
keel săzh' noo yă.
que n. n. agenouillassions.
kuh noo noo zăzh noo yă see ōn.
que v. v. agenouillassiez.
kuh voo voo zăzh' noo yă see a.
qu'ils s'agenouillassent.
keel săzh' noo yăss'.

Que je m'ennuyasse.
kuh zh' măn nŭ ee yăss'.
que tu t'ennuyasses.
kuh tū tăn nŭ ee yăss'.
qu'il s'ennuyât.
keel săn nŭ ee yă.
que n. n. ennuyassions.
kuh noo noo zăn nŭ ee yă see ōn.
que v. v. ennuyassiez.
kuh voo voo săn nŭ ee yă see a.
qu'ils s'ennuyassent.
keel săn nŭ ee yăss'.

REFLECTIVE VERBS,— *SE RECUEILLIR*, to col-
suh r' kuh yeer.
lect one's-self, to meditate, AND *S'ASSEOIR*, to sit
să swehr.
down.

Infinitif Présent,	Se recueillir.	S'asseoir.
	suh r' kuh yeer.	să swehr.
Participe Présent,	Se recueillant.	S'asseyant.
	suh r' kuh yăn.	sa seh yăn.
Passé,	Recueilli.	Assis.
	r' kuh yee.	ă see.

INDICATIF.
Présent.

Je me recueille.
zhuh m' ruh kuhy'.
tu te recueilles.
tū t' ruh kuhy'.
il se recueille.
eel suh r' kuhy'.
nous nous recueillons.
noo noo r' kuh yōn.
vous vous recueillez.
voo voo 'r' kuh ya.
ils se recueillent.
eel suh r' kuhy'.

Je m'assieds.
zh' mă see a.
tu t'assieds.
tū tă see a.
il s'assied.
eel să see a.
nous nous asseyons.
noo noo să seh yōn.
vous vous asseyez.
voo voo să seh ya.
ils s'asseyent.
eel să sĕhy'.

Imparfait.

Je me recueillais.
zhuh m' ruh kuh yeh.
tu te recueillais.
tü t' ruh kuh yeh.
il se recueillait.
eel suh r' kuh yeh.
nous nous recueillions.
noo noo r' kuh yee oñ.
vous vous recueilliez.
voo voo r' kuh yee a.
ils se recueillaient.
eel suh r' kuh yŏh.

Je m'asseyais.
zh' mă seh yeh.
tu t'asseyais.
tü tă seh yeh.
il s'asseyait.
eel să seh yeh.
nous nous asseyions.
noo noo să seh yee oñ.
vous vous asseyiez.
voo voo să seh yee a.
ils s'asseyaient.
eel să seh yŏh.

Passé défini.

Je me recueillis.
zhuh m' ruh kuh yee.
tu te recueillis.
tü t' ruh kuh yee.
il se recueillit.
eel suh r' kuh yee.
nous nous recueillîmes.
noo noo r' kuh yeem'.
vous vous recueillîtes.
voo voo r' kuh yeet'.
ils se recueillirent.
eel suh r' kuh yeer.

Je m'assis.
zh' mă see.
tu t'assis.
tü tă see.
il s'assit.
eel să see.
nous nous assîmes.
noo noo să seem'.
vous vous assîtes.
voo voo să seet'.
ils s'assirent.
eel să seer'.

Futur simple.

Je me recueillerai.
zhuh m' ruh kuhy' ra.
tu te recueilleras.
tü t' ruh kuhy' ră.
il se recueillera.
eel suh r' kuhy' ră.
nous nous recueillerons.
noo noo r' kuhy' roñ.
vous vous recueillerez.
voo voo r' kuhy' ra.
ils se recueilleront.
eel suh r' kuhy' roñ.

Je m'assiérai.
zh' mă see a ra.
tu t'assiéras.
tü tă see a ră.
il s'assiéra.
eel să see a ră.
nous nous assiérons.
noo noo să see a roñ.
vous vous assiérez.
voo voo să see a ra.
ils s'assiéront.
eel să see a roñ.

CONDITIONNEL.
Présent.

Je me recueillerais.
zhuh m' ruh kuhy' reh.

tu te recueillerais.
tü t' ruh kuhy' reh.

il se recueillerait.
eel suh r' kuhy' reh.

nous nous recueillerions.
noo noo r' kuh yuh ree ōn.

vous vous recueilleriez.
voo voo r' kuh yuh ree a.

ils se recueilleraient.
eel suh r' kuhy rĕh.

Je m'assiérais.
zh' mă see a reh.

tu t'assiérais.
tü tă see a reh.

il s'assiérait.
eel să see a reh.

nous nous assiérions.
noo noo să see a ree ōn.

vous vous assiériez.
voo voo ză see a ree a.

ils s'assiéraient
eel să see a rĕh.

IMPÉRATIF.

Recueille-toi.
r' kuhy' tweh.

qu'il se recueille.
keel suh r' kuhy'.

recueillons-nous.
r' kuh yōn noo.

recueillez-vous.
r' kuh ya voo.

qu'ils se recueillent.
keel suh r' kuhy'.

Assieds-toi.
ă see a tweh.

qu'il s'asseye.
keel să sehy'.

asseyons-nous.
ă seh yōn noo.

asseyez-vous.
ă seh ya voo.

qu'ils s'asseyent.
keel să sĕhy'.

SUBJONCTIF.
Présent.

Que je me recueille.
kuh zh' muh r' kuhy'.

que tu te recueilles.
kuh tü t' ruh kuhy'.

qu'il se recueille.
keel suh r' kuhy'.

que nous nous recueillions.
kuh noo noo r' kuh yee ōn.

que vous vous recueilliez.
kuh voo voo r' kuh yee a.

qu'ils se recueillent.
keel suh r' kuhy'.

Que je m'asseye.
kuh zh' mă sehy'.

que tu t'asseyes.
kuh tü tă sehy.

qu'il s'asseye.
keel să sehy'.

que nous nous asseyions.
kuh noo noo za seh yee ōn.

que vous vous asseyiez.
kuh voo voo ză seh yee a.

qu'ils s'asseyent.
keel să sĕhy.

Imparfait.

Que je me recueillisse.	**Que je m'assisse.**
kuh zh' muh r' kuh yeess'.	kuh zh' mă seess'.
que tu te recueillisses.	que tu t'assisses.
kuh tü t' ruh kuh yeess'.	kuh tü tă seess'.
qu'il se recueillît.	qu'il s'assît.
keel suh r' kuh yee.	keel să see.
que n. n. recueillissions.	que nous nous assissions.
kuh noo noo r' kuh yee see ōn.	kuh noo neo ză see see ōn.
que v. v. recueillissiez.	que vous vous assissiez.
kuh voo voo r' kuh yee see a.	kuh voo voo ză see see a.
qu'ils se recueillissent.	qu'ils s'assissent.
keel suh r' kuh yeess'.	keel să seess'.

IRREGULAR VERBS, — *VOULOIR*, to be willing, to
voo lwer.

wish, AND *PEINDRE*, to paint.
pīndr'.

Infinitif Présent,	**Vouloir.**	**Peindre.**
	voo lwer.	pīndr'.
Participe Présent,	**Voulant.**	**Peignant.**
	voo lān.	peh gñān.
Passé,	**Voulu.**	**Peint.**
	voo lü.	pīn.

INDICATIF.
Présent.

Je veux.	**Je peins.**
zh' veū.	zh' pīn.
tu veux.	tu peins.
tü veū.	tü pīn.
il veut.	il peint.
eel veū.	eel pīn.
nous voulons.	nous peignons.
noo voo lōn.	noo peh gñōn.
vous voulez.	vous peignez.
voo voo la.	voo peh gña.
ils veulent.	ils peignent.
eel vuhl'.	eel pehgñ'.

APPENDIX.

Imparfait.

Je voulais.
zh' voo leh.
tu voulais.
tü voo leh.
il voulait.
eel voo leh.
nous voulions.
noo voo lee ōn.
vous vouliez.
voo voo lee a.
ils voulaient.
eel voo leh.

Je peignais.
zh' peh g͞neh.
tu peignais.
tü peh g͞neh.
il peignait.
eel peh g͞neh.
nous peignions.
noo peh g͞nee ōn.
vous peigniez.
voo peh g͞nee a.
ils peignaient.
eel peh g͞neh.

Passé défini.

Je voulus.
zh' voo lü.
tu voulus.
tü voo lü.
il voulut.
eel voo lü.
nous voulûmes.
noo voo lüm'.
vous voulûtes.
voo voo lüt'.
ils voulurent.
eel voo lür'.

Je peignis.
zh' peh g͞nee.
tu peignis.
tü peh g͞nee.
il peignit.
eel peh g͞nee.
nous peignîmes.
noo peh g͞neem'.
vous peignîtes.
voo peh g͞neet'.
ils peignirent.
eel peh g͞neer'.

Futur simple.

Je voudrai.
zh' voo dra.
tu voudras.
tü voo drä.
il voudra.
eel voo drä.
nous voudrons.
noo voo drōn.
vous voudrez.
voo voo dra.
ils voudront.
eel voo drōn.

Je peindrai.
zh' pin dra.
tu peindras.
tü pin drä.
il peindra.
eel pin drä.
nous peindrons.
noo pin drōn.
vous peindrez.
voo pin dra.
ils peindront.
eel pin drōn.

CONDITIONNEL.

Présent.

Je voudrais.
zh' voo dreh.
tu voudrais.
tü voo dreh.
il voudrait.
eel voo dreh.
nous voudrions.
noo voo dree ōn.
vous voudriez.
voo voo dree a.
ils voudraient.
eel voo drĕh.

Je peindrais.
zh' pĩn dreh.
tu peindrais.
tü pĩn dreh.
il peindrait.
eel pĩn dreh.
nous peindrions.
noo pĩn dree ōn.
vous peindriez.
voo pĩn dree a.
ils peindraient.
eel pĩn drĕh.

IMPÉRATIF.

[person).
Veuillez (*is the only*
vuh ja.

Peins.
pĩn.
qu'il peigne.
keel pehg͞n'.
peignons.
peh g͞nōn.
peignez.
peh g͞na.
qu'ils peignent.
keel pĕhg͞n'.

SUBJONCTIF.

Présent.

Que je veuille.
kuh zh' vuhy'.
que tu veuilles.
kuh tü vuhy'.
qu'il veuille.
keel vuhy'.
que nous voulions.
kuh noo voo lee ōn.
que vous vouliez.
kuh voo voo lee a.
qu'ils veuillent.
keel vuhy'.

Que je peigne.
kuh zh' pehg͞n'.
que tu peignes.
kuh tü pehg͞n'.
qu'il peigne.
keel pehg͞n'.
que nous peignions.
kuh noo peh g͞nee ōn.
que vous peigniez.
kuh voo peh g͞nee a.
qu'ils peignent.
keel pĕhg͞n.

Imparfait.

Que je voulusse.
kuh zh' voo lüss'.
que tu voulusses.
küh tü voo lüss'.
qu'il voulût.
keel voo lü.
que nous voulussions.
kuh noo voo lü see ōn.
que vous voulussiez.
kuh voo voo lü see a.
qu'ils voulussent.
keel voo lüss'.

Que je peignisse.
küh zh' peh gñeess'.
que tu peignisses.
kuh tü peh gñeess'.
qu'il peignît.
keel peh gñee.
que nous peignissions.
kuh noo peh gñee see ōn.
que vous peignissiez.
kuh voo peh gñee see a.
qu'ils peignissent.
keel peh gñeess'.

THE MARSEILLAISE HYMN.

I.

Come, our country's sons!
The day of glory is here.
Against us Tyranny
Lifts her bloody standard, —
Lifts her bloody standard.
Hear ye in the plains
The roar of the fierce soldiers?
They are coming, even within your arms,
To murder your sons, your wives!
To arms, citizens!
Form your battalions!
March! Let us march! let their polluted blood
Water our furrows!

II.

What means this horde of slaves,
Of traitors, of confederate kings?
For whom are these ignominious fetters,
These irons, long since prepared, —
These irons, long since prepared?
Frenchmen! for us! Ah, what an outrage
What transports should it raise!
It is we whom they dare threaten
To reduce to ancient slavery!
    To arms, &c.

III.

What! shall foreign cohorts
Give us law on our own hearthstones?
What! shall mercenary legions
Vanquish our proud warriors, —
Vanquish our proud warriors?
Great God! by fettered hands
Shall our necks be bent to the yoke?
Shall base despots become
The masters of our fate?
    To arms, &c.

IV.

Tremble, tyrants! and you, ye perjured!
Scorn of every party,
Tremble! your parricidal schemes
Shall at last have their reward, —
Shall at last have their reward.
Every thing is arming to combat you:
If they fall, our young heroes,
France will bring forth others
Ready to fight against you.
  To arms, &c.

V.

Frenchmen! like generous warriors,
Strike or forbear to strike!
Spare those sad victims
Who are sorrowfully arming against us, —
Who are sorrowfully arming against us;
But the sanguinary despot,
But the accomplice of Bouillé, —
All the tigers who without pity
Rend the bosom of their mother, —
  To arms, &c.

VI.

Sacred love of country,
Guide, sustain, our avenging arms:
Liberty, beloved Liberty,
Fight on the side of thy defenders, —
Fight on the side of thy defenders.
Under our banners let victory
Rally to thy deep tones;
Let thine expiring enemies
See thy triumph and our glory.
To arms, citizens!
Form your battalions!
March! Let us march! let their polluted blood
Water our furrows!

LA MARSEILLAISE.
lă măr seh yehz'.

PREMIER COUPLET.

ALLONS, enfans de la patrie !
ă lōñ zāñ fāñ duh lă pă tree !

Le jour de gloire est arrivé.
luh zhoor duh glwehr eh tă ree va.

Contre nous de la tyrannie,
kōñ truh noo duh lă tee ră nee,

L'étendard sanglant est levé,
la tāñ dăr sāñ glāñ teh luh va,

L'étendard sanglant est levé.
la tāñ dăr sāñ glāñ teh luh va.

Entendez-vous dans les campagnes
āñ tāñ da voo dāñ la kāñ păgñ'

Mugir ces féroces soldats ?
mŭ zheer sa fa rŏ suh sŏl dă ?

Ils viennent, jusques dans vos bras,
eel vee ehnuh, zhŭss kuh dāñ vo bră,

Egorger vos fils, vos compagnes !
a gor zha vo feess, vo kōñ păgñ !

Aux armes, citoyens !
ŏ zăr muh, see tweh yīñ !

Formez vos bataillons :
for ma vo bă tă yōñ :

Marchez ! marchons ! qu'un sang impur
măr sha ! măr shōñ ! kūñ sāñ kīñ pŭr

Abreuve nos sillons !
ă bruh vuh no see yōñ !

DEUXIÈME COUPLET.

Que veut cette horde d'esclaves,
kuh veū seh tuh ŏrduh da sklahv',

De traîtres, de rois conjurés !
duh treh truh, duh rweh kōñ zhŭ ra !

Pour qui ces ignobles entraves,
poor keĕ sa zee gñŏ bluh zāñ trăv',

Ces fers, dès longtemps préparés,
sa fehr, deh lōñ tāñ pra pă ra,

APPENDIX. 167

Ces fers, dès longtemps préparés ?
sa fehr, deh lōñ tāñ pra pā ra?

Français ! pour nous, ah ! quel outrage!
frāñ seh! poor noo, ah! kehl oo trāzh!

Quels transports il doit exciter !
kehl trāñss por zeel dweh tak see ta!

C'est nous qu'on ose menacer
seh noo kōñ no zūh muh nā sa

De rendre à l'antique esclavage !
duh rāñ dr' ā lāñ teek' a sklā vāzh!

    Aux armes, &c.
    ō zār muh, &c.

TROISIÈME COUPLET.

Quoi ! des cohortes étrangères
kweh! da kō ōr tuh za trāñ zhehr

Feraient la loi dans nos foyers ?
fuh reh lā lweh dāñ no fweh ya?

Quoi ! ces phalanges mercenaires
kweh! sa fā lāñ zhuh mehr suh nehr'

Terrasseraient nos fiers guerriers ?
ta rā suh reh no fee ehr ğa ree a?

Terrasseraient nos fiers guerriers ?
ta ra suh reh no fee ehr ğa ree a?

Grand Dieu ! par des mains enchaînées
ğrāñ dee ēū! pār da miñ zāñ sheh na

Nos fronts sous le joug se ploieraient !
no frōñ soo luh zhoo suh plweh reh!

De vils despotes deviendraient
duh veel dehss pō tuh duh vee iñ dreh,

Les maîtres de nos destinées !
la mēh truh duh no dehss tee na!

    Aux armes, &c.
    ō zār muh, &c.

QUATRIÈME COUPLET.

Tremblez, tyrans ! et vous perfides !
trāñ bla, tee rāñ! za voo pehr feed!

L'opprobre de tous les partis,
lō prō bruh duh too la pār tee,

Tremblez ! vos projets parricides
trāñ bla! vō prō zheh pā ree see d'

Vont enfin recevoir leur prix,
vōñ tāñ fiñ ruh suh vwehr luhr pree,

Vont enfin recevoir leur prix.
vōn tān fin ruh suh vwehr luhr pree.

Tout est soldat pour vous combattre ;
too teh sŏl dă poor voo kōn bătr';

S'ils tombent, nos jeunes héros,
seel tōn buh, nŏ zhuh nuh a rŏ,

La France en produit de nouveaux
lă frān s'ān prŏ dŭ ee duh noo vŏ

Contre vous tous prêts à se battre.
kōn truh voo tooss prĕh ză suh bătr'.

  Aux armes, &c.
  ŏ zăr muh, &c.

CINQUIÈME COUPLET.

Français ! en guerriers magnanimes,
frān seh! sān ğa ree a mă ğnă neem',

Portez ou retenez vos coups ;
pŏr ta zoo ruh tuh na vŏ koo;

Epargnez ces tristes victimes
a păr ğna sa treess tuh veek teem'

A regret s'armant contre nous,
ă ruh ğreh săr mān kōn truh voo,

A regret s'armant contre nous ;
ă ruh ğreh săr mān kōn truh voo;

Mais le despote sanguinaire,
meh luh dehs pŏ tuh sān ğee nehr',

Mais le complice de Bouillé —
meh luh kōn plee suh duh boo ya —

Tous ces tigres qui sans pitié,
too sa tee ğruh kee sān pee tee a,

Déchirent le sein de leur mère !
da shee ruh luh sīn duh luhr mehr'!

  Aux armes, &c.
  ŏ zăr muh, &c.

SIXIÈME COUPLET.

Amour sacré de la patrie,
ă moor sa kra duh lă pă tree,

Conduis, soutiens nos bras vengeurs :
kōn dŭ ee, soo tee īn no bră vān zhuhr:

Liberté, Liberté chérie,
lee behr ta, lee behr ta sha ree,

Combats avec tes défenseurs,
kōn bă ză vehk ta da fān suhr,

APPENDIX.

Combats avec tes défenseurs ;
kōn bă ză vehk ta da fān suhr;

Sous nos drapeaux que la victoire
soo no dră po kuh lă veek twehr

Accoure à tes mâles accents ;
ă koor' ă ta măh luh zăk sān;

Que tes ennemis expirans
kuh ta zeh nuh mee zaks pee rān

Voient ton triomphe et notre gloire.
vweh tōn tree ōnf' a nŏ truh glwehr.

Aux armes, citoyens !
ŏ zăr muh, see tweh yīn!

Formez vos bataillons :
for ma vo bă tă yōn:

Marchez ! marchons ! qu'un sang impur
măr sha! măr shōn! kūn sān kīn pŭr

Abreuve nos sillons !
ă bruh vuh no see yōn!

LA MARSEILLAISE.

ROUGET DE LISLE.

OBSERVATION. — In singing, as well as in reading, each syllable must be distinctly uttered. This rule is still more binding in singing as there is no semi-mute syllables. All songs (written in good French), whatever their character may otherwise be, are pronounced similar to the "Marseillaise."

NOTE. — The student will observe the difference in the pronunciation of the "Marseillaise" when read, and its pronunciation when sung. The same principles of pronunciation must be applied to all songs.

Lightning Source UK Ltd.
Milton Keynes UK
UKHW021132201020
371904UK00004B/353